Explore

Common Core/ PARCC Prep
Grade 3 Reading

by Dr. James E. Swalm and Dr. June I. Coultas

with Patricia Braccio and Kathleen Haughey
Edited by Ralph Kantrowitz and Sarah M.W. Espano

Queue, Inc • 80 Hathaway Drive • Stratford CT 06615
Phone 800 232 2224 • Fax 800 775 2729

www.qworkbooks.com

The Authors

Dr. James Swalm has been actively involved in the development of classroom instructional materials for many years. As Director of the New Jersey Right to Read and Bureau of Basic Skills, he participated in the development of statewide tests in reading, writing and mathematics as well as in the writing of various instructional and staff development materials in reading and language arts. Dr. Swalm has authored and co-authored numerous books and professional articles on reading, writing, and assessment, as well as on the use of technology in instruction. He has taught both undergraduate and graduate level courses in reading and curriculum development, and at all levels, K–12. Dr. Swalm has also been a principal, assistant superintendent, and superintendent, and has served as an educational consultant to many school districts.

Dr. June I. Coultas is well-known in the field of education and curriculum development. Her many positions include that of teacher, director of curriculum and instruction, college professor, consultant, lecturer, and award-winning grant writer. She is the author and co-author of numerous educational books, as well as of multimedia software programs. Her career includes being New Jersey director of the federal Right-to-Read Program, and manager of the state Bureau of Basic Skills. In addition to memberships in numerous professional associations, she is a past president of the New Jersey Reading Association.

Acknowledgments
Illustrations
Carl W. Swanson, Ph.D.
Maureen B. Coultas
Sarah J. Holden

Poems
Glenn G. Coats, M. Ed.
Jonathan D. Kantrowitz

Student Book ISBN: 978-1-4973-3767-1 • Class Pack ISBN: 978-0-7827-2337-3 • Copyright © 2014 Queue, Inc. Whiteboard/Workbook Class Pack ISBN: 978-0-7827-2543-8 • Standalone Whiteboard ISBN: 978-0-7827-2542-1

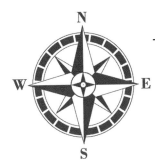

Table of Contents

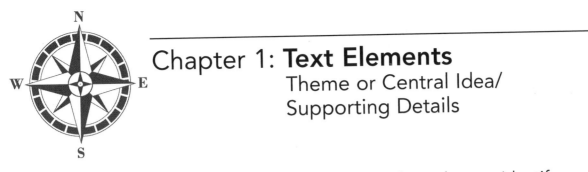
When reading a story or passage, it is important to know how to identify central ideas, supporting details and theme. It is helpful to understand these terms. Once you have learned about the terms, it will be easier to find them in the passages and stories.

Every passage you will read in this book will have a central idea and usually a theme. Many of the questions you will be asked will have to do with identifying the central idea or theme.

RL.3.2, RI.3.2: RECOGNITION OF CENTRAL IDEA OR THEME

You Try It

You have just finished reading a story. Your teacher asks you to write a sentence or paragraph stating what the theme of the story is. How do you know what the theme is?

- Do you just rewrite the story?

- Do you tell your teacher what happened in the story?

- Do you think about what the story was trying to say?

Your best bet would be to think about what was the moral or lesson in the story. Think about why the story was written.

What is a central idea?

The **central idea** is the "big idea" in the passage or what the passage is mostly about.

"**Central**" means most important, or main.

"**Idea**" means a thought, or point.

Therefore, the central idea is the most important idea in a passage or story.

HERE ARE SOME WAYS TO FIND THE CENTRAL IDEA
- Look at each sentence in the passage or story and think about whether or not it is important to the story as a whole. Would the passage change if this sentence was not there?
- Try to write a headline of less than 5 words to sum up what the passage says.

What is a theme?

A **theme** is an idea that flows through a reading passage or a book and says something about life.

Popular themes are topics that everyone is interested in.

They make reading enjoyable and fun.

Here are 3 examples of themes:
- Believe in Yourself
- Accept Others' Differences
- Try New Things

HERE ARE SOME WAYS TO FIND THE THEME
- Look at the title. Sometimes it tells you a lot about the theme.
- Notice the details. What greater meaning might they have? This larger meaning is the theme.

RL.3.1, RI.3.1: RECOGNITION OF SUPPORTING DETAILS

What are supporting details?

Supporting details are ideas or sentences that build upon or explain the central idea.

To get the point across, an author uses details to explain his or her point of view.

These details could be facts or additional parts of the story that build upon the idea.

It is usually best to find the central idea first; that will make it easier to determine which sentences include the supporting details.

HERE IS AN EXAMPLE TO SHOW SUPPORTING DETAILS

Read the paragraph below.

> Elephants are extremely large animals. In fact, the elephant is the largest animal on land. Some male elephants can grow to be thirteen feet tall. That's probably twice as tall as either of your parents. Elephants can weigh between 10,000 and 14,000 pounds. That's as much as a garbage truck!

The central idea of this paragraph is that elephants are large animals.

The supporting details are:
• Elephants are the largest animals on land.
• Elephants can grow to be thirteen feet tall.
• Elephants can weigh between 10,000 and 14,000 pounds.

LET'S TRY IT TOGETHER

> **DIRECTIONS:**   Read the story below and we'll discuss the questions together.

The Wind and the Sun

from Aesop's Fables

The Wind and the Sun were disputing which was the stronger. Suddenly they saw a traveler coming down the road, and the Sun said: "I see a way to decide our dispute. Whichever of us can cause that traveler to take off his cloak shall be regarded as the stronger. You begin." So the Sun retired behind a cloud, and the Wind began to blow as hard as it could upon the traveler. But the harder he blew, the more closely did the traveler wrap his cloak round him, till at last the Wind had to give up in despair. Then the Sun came out and shone in all his glory upon the traveler, who soon found it too hot to walk with his cloak on. ■

What is the central idea?

Is it that the Sun and the Wind were fighting?
No, that is not the central idea. Although it is a large part of the story, it does not tell us what the entire story is about.

Is it that there is traveler coming down the road?
The fact that there is a traveler in the story is a supporting detail. However, it is not the central idea.

Is it that the traveler was wearing a cloak?
The fact that the traveler is wearing a cloak is another supporting detail, not the central idea.

Is it that the Sun is more powerful than the Wind?
Yes! That is the central idea of the story. If you look at the entire story, you will notice that all of the details go back to and support this idea

What is the theme?

Is it that the forces of nature are very powerful?
No. Although the passage does seem to explain that the forces of nature are powerful, that is not the theme.

Is it that it is better to be cold than to be warm?
No. Although the passage does talk about being cold and being warm, that is not the theme.

Is it that kindness gets better results than force?
Yes! That is the theme of the story. Overall, the story is demonstrating that the Sun gets better results because it is being kind, while the Wind is being forceful.

What are the supporting details?

Let's use a graphic organizer to sort out the supporting details from this story.

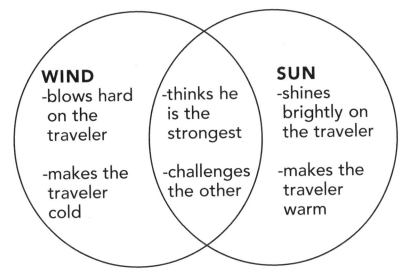

WIND
-blows hard on the traveler

-makes the traveler cold

-thinks he is the strongest

-challenges the other

SUN
-shines brightly on the traveler

-makes the traveler warm

5

YOU TRY IT

A Daring Feat

CLINK — CRASH!

Barry stood there bug-eyed, mouth open, and unable to speak. He stared at the white tablecloth that hung limply from his right hand. At his feet and scattered for some distance over the garage floor lay pieces of glass. Barry stared, dumbfounded. What had gone wrong?

As far as Barry could tell, he had performed the trick the way he had seen it done on TV. The Great Harrington had set a table with good china plates, glasses, and silverware. With one quick motion, he had pulled the white tablecloth from under them. While the objects had moved slightly, everything had remained on the table—unbroken.

For his birthday, Barry's aunt had given him a magic set. It contained a top hat, a magic wand, cards, coins, and colorful handkerchiefs. Barry had learned all the tricks in a book that accompanied the magic set. He enjoyed performing those tricks for his family and friends. However, eventually everyone got tired of seeing the same tricks performed over and over again. He needed to learn some new ones.

✔ **CHECKING FOR UNDERSTANDING**

What had Barry probably done right before the story began?

Anytime there was a special on TV featuring a magician, Barry watched intently as each trick was performed. Obviously, he wasn't going to saw a woman in half. He didn't have a suitable trunk for the trick, and besides, his sister refused to be part of the act. Making a rabbit or a dove appear was a possibility, however. That is, until his parents objected to keeping more animals in the house.

When Barry tried to teach Skeeter, their big, fuzzy sheepdog, a few tricks, Skeeter treated it all like a game. He kept bounding around, running off with props and washing Barry's face with his long tongue. Barry then tried putting their cat, Muffin, in a box for a trick. However, her constant meowing made the trick impossible. Quickly Barry had opened the lid. Muffin had leaped out and dashed for a safe hiding place. Barry knew that Skeeter and Muffin couldn't be counted on to star in a show. So much for animal magic tricks!

Barry was getting discouraged about adding new tricks until he saw the Great Harrington's tablecloth trick. That looked like something he could do. It seemed simple enough and the props were easy to find. He had set up a card table and covered it with an old tablecloth. Instead of real dishes and glasses, he began with paper plates and cups. However, they didn't work. The paper plates and cups were too light and bounced around. He realized he would have to use real dishes.

Hmmm, where to get the dishes? Barry was smart enough not to use any of his family's good dishes. However, his sister's glass tea set would be perfect. She no longer played with it.

Only now, the tea set lay in dozens of pieces on the garage floor. Not a single piece was unbroken. Barry got a broom and dustpan and began cleaning up the broken glass. He wondered how his sister would take the news about her tea set. Maybe she wouldn't be too upset. He might only get a lecture from his parents about taking the tea set without asking permission, if he were lucky. But, Barry couldn't count on that. He would probably have to dip into his savings and buy her something.

What was he going to do about his magic trick? As the last of the glass went into the garbage, Barry decided to use only unbreakable props in the future. At least, that is, until he mastered "The Gravity Defying Tablecloth Trick." ∎

1. **How did Barry learn about the tablecloth trick?**

   A His sister took him to a magic show.

   B His aunt told him about the trick.

   C He read about the trick in a book.

   D He watched a TV show about magic.

HELPFUL HINT
This question asks you to think about a detail from the story. Do you remember when Barry learned the trick? Reread the first five paragraphs of the story if you can't recall.

2. **Who bought Barry a magic set for his birthday?**

   A his mother

   B his father

   C his aunt

   D his sister

HELPFUL HINT
This question asks you to identify a detail in the story. Barry got a magic set for his birthday. Who gave it to him? If needed, reread the beginning of the story to refresh your memory.

3. **Why did Barry want to learn a new trick?**

   A His friends and family wanted him to enter a magic show.

   B His friends and family were tired of seeing the same tricks.

   C He had seen a TV program about the Great Harrington.

   D He wanted to grow up to be like the Great Harrington.

HELPFUL HINT
This question asks you to find a supporting detail from the story. If you are unsure of the answer, skim the story and look for the detail.

4. **Why couldn't Barry use his pets in his tricks?**

    A   They wouldn't do what he told them to do.

    B   They were too big to fit inside his box.

    C   They wouldn't stop making loud sounds.

    D   They kept trying to find a place to hide.

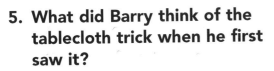

HELPFUL HINT
This question also asks you to identify a supporting detail in the story. Barry tried to do tricks with both his dog and cat. What happened in both instances?

5. **What did Barry think of the tablecloth trick when he first saw it?**

    A   He thought that trick seemed silly.

    B   He thought the trick looked easy.

    C   He thought the trick took time to learn.

    D   He thought the trick used a lot of dishes.

HELPFUL HINT
This question asks you to recall Barry's first reaction when he saw the tablecloth trick. What was his attitude about it before he tried it? Reread the early paragraphs of the story if you are unsure.

6. **Why might Barry's sister be mad at him?**

    A   He wouldn't let her help.

    B   He didn't master the trick.

    C   He used her cat for a trick.

    D   He broke her glass tea set.

HELPFUL HINT
This question asks you to draw a conclusion. Is there anything that Barry did in the story that might have upset his sister?

FOR THE OPEN-ENDED QUESTION BELOW, REMEMBER TO:
- Pay attention to what the question is asking you.
- Be sure to answer everything the question asks you.
- Fully explain what you mean by your answer.
- Use details from the story.

7. **Think about how the events in the story show what kind of a person Barry is. Based on your reading, list some specific details about Barry's character. Be sure to give supporting details from the story to support your answer.**

_____

_____

_____

_____

_____

_____

_____

_____

_____

_____

_____

_____

_____

YOU TRY IT

DIRECTIONS:	Read this story, and answer the questions that follow.
INTRODUCTION:	A class decides to hold a fund-raiser to help one of their classmates. Read how they plan to raise the money.

Magic Show Memo

To: All Teachers
Re: Magic Show
From: Mrs. Jones's Fourth Grade

Our class has decided to hold a Magic Show to raise money for the Dashawn Fund. As you know, Dashawn is a fourth-grade student in our class. He was seriously hurt a month ago when he fell off his bike. Money from this event will be used to help pay for the costs of Dashawn's operations.

One of our parents, Mr. Williams, is a performing magician. He has volunteered to teach the students in our class to do magic tricks. The students and Mr. Williams have been spending several nights a week for the past month practicing for the show. Mr. Williams says he has never seen a more talented group of amateur magicians.

> ✔ **CHECKING FOR UNDERSTANDING**
> Why did Mrs. Jones's class decide to put on this magic show?

We are inviting all students and their families to attend our evening performance. Come watch the students from Mrs. Jones's class perform their magic. Everyone who attends will have a great time. Where else can you see fellow students do mystifying tricks?

4 Tickets go on sale starting March 10th during lunch. Anyone wishing to purchase a ticket should bring his or her money to the cafeteria at lunch. A parent from Mrs. Jones's class will be selling tickets in the cafeteria each day until March 17th, the day of the performance. Tickets can also be purchased after school in the school office or on the night of the performance.

Attached is a flier announcing the magic show. Please post this in your classrooms. Thank you for your support for our important project.

Sincerely, Mrs. Jones's Class

COME ONE, COME ALL!

SEE THE
GREAT WILLIAMS MAGIC TROUPE
PERFORM MAGIC NEVER BEFORE
SEEN ON THIS CONTINENT

The Great Williams Magic Troupe is known the world over for its magic. Everyone who has seen them raves about their mystifying magic. Don't miss the only performance being given in our area. You will have an exciting and suspense-filled time.

DATE: March 17

TIME: 7:30 P.M.

PLACE: Field Elementary School Gymnasium

COST

Before March 17th
$1.00 per student
$3.00 per family

Night of the Performance
$2.00 per student
$5.00 per family

Magic Tricks will include:

- The Card that Whispers
- The Lady that Floats
- The Disappearing Knots
- Predict-a-Card
- Gobble the Grape
- Mind Reading
- The Handkerchief that Appears and Disappears

1. Why did the author *most likely* write the memo?

   A to ask teachers and students to be in the magic show

   B to ask teachers to tell their students about the magic show

   C to show teachers and students where to learn magic tricks

   D to tell teachers and students how to put on a magic show

HELPFUL HINT

This question asks you to think about why the teacher decided to contact her fellow teachers. What did she ask the teachers to do after they had read the memo?

2. How long have the students been practicing for the show?

   A several days

   B one week

   C several hours

   D one month

HELPFUL HINT

This is a question about supporting details. Mrs. Jones talked about the efforts of her class. Reread the second paragraph and look for how long they have been getting ready.

3. What does the word "purchase" mean in paragraph four of the memo?

   A buy

   B find

   C give

   D try

HELPFUL HINT

This question asks you to select the meaning of the underlined word. Reread the sentence that uses the the word "purchase." Are there any clues to the word's meaning?

4. **Why does the author include a flier with the memo?**

   A so the students will take it home to their parents

   B so the teachers will put it up in their classrooms

   C so the students will take it to their neighbors

   D so the teachers will put it up around their town

⭐ **HELPFUL HINT**
This question asks you to make a judgment. Why is the flier important to getting the message out?

5. **Why should students buy tickets before the night of the performance?**

   A The tickets might all be sold by the night of the performance.

   B Students won't get good seats if they wait to buy the tickets.

   C The tickets won't cost as much if they are bought early.

   D Students' tickets will be as much as adult tickets the night of the performance.

⭐ **HELPFUL HINT**
This question asks you to draw a conclusion. Anywhere in the passage, was there a mention of why it would be better to buy ahead of time?

6. **Why does the flier *most likely* include a list of tricks that will be performed?**

   A so students won't be scared by the tricks

   B so students will get excited about the show

   C so parents will want to go see the show

   D so parents won't be surprised by the tricks

⭐ **HELPFUL HINT**
This question asks you to make a judgment about why the author decided to do something. If you had written the flier, would you have included a list of tricks? Why?

FOR THE OPEN-ENDED QUESTION BELOW, REMEMBER TO:
• Pay attention to what the question is asking you.
• Be sure to answer everything the question asks you.
• Fully explain what you mean by your answer.
• Use details from the story.

7. Explain the purpose of the first paragraph of the flier.

YOU TRY IT

> **DIRECTIONS:** Read this passage, and answer the questions that follow.

Animal Acts

For many people, the most enjoyable part of a trip to the circus is seeing the acts that involve animals. If you are included in that group, you can thank Henri Martin. In 1831, wild animal acts became part of the circus. He worked with lions, boa snakes, elephants, and other animals. His act was in Paris, France. Then, animal acts were parts of plays.

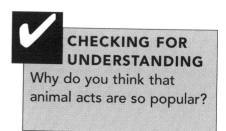

CHECKING FOR UNDERSTANDING
Why do you think that animal acts are so popular?

All animals were not trained in the same way. Some were treated cruelly. Trainers wanted the animals to fear them. Clyde Beatty was one of those. He worked with forty lions and tigers at one time.

Others used gentle but firm methods. They did not hurt their animals. Lipizzaner horses are used in many circuses. They are those white horses bareback

riders use. These animals are very smart. They are trained carefully and don't fear their trainers.

Some trainers work with only one type of animal. Not the Knie family of Switzerland! They used polar bears, giraffes, and camels. They even used had hippos and rhinos.

Which animal is the most dangerous? Circus people say it is the elephant mostly because of its size and strength. It may also be because of the kind of acts elephants do. They use their trunks to lift people onto their backs.

People stand in front of them as they

stand on their hind legs. Some people even stand on elephants' knees. One false move, though, and a person could be hurt.

Animal acts often come from certain countries. Many bareback riders are English. Wild animal acts are from Germany. Some are also from the United States. Sticking your head in a lion's mouth takes courage. An American was the first to do it. His name was Isaac Van Amburg.

Some circus families go back many years. Children learn to be in an act with their parents. It takes years of training for an act to become part of the circus. ■

1. What is this passage *mostly* about?

   A people who train animals and how they do it

   B circus families who perform for years and years

   C animals that perform in circuses

   D the most dangerous animals in the world

HELPFUL HINT
This question asks you to think about what this passage is really about. What do you think the author was trying to say when he or she wrote this passage?

2. Why are Lipizzaner horses used in many circuses?

   A They are white horses.

   B They are very smart.

   C They are very dangerous.

   D They are afraid of their trainers.

HELPFUL HINT
This question asks you to recall information stated during the passage. If you are unsure of the answer, reread the third paragraph.

3. Which animal is the *most* dangerous?

   A a lion

   B a tiger

   C a polar bear

   D an elephant

HELPFUL HINT
This question asks you to find a supporting detail from the passage. If you are unsure of the answer, look back in the passage for a mention of a dangerous animal.

4. **What does the word "cruelly" mean in the following sentences: "All animals were not trained the same. Some were treated cruelly. Trainers wanted the animals to fear them"?**

   A lightly

   B fairly

   C harshly

   D fearfully

HELPFUL HINT
This question asks you to select the meaning of the word "cruelly." Are there any clues in the other sentences to let you know the word's meaning?

5. **The man who first stuck his head in a lion's mouth was**

   A English.

   B German.

   C French.

   D American.

HELPFUL HINT
This question also asks you to find a Supporting detail from the story. If you are unsure of the answer, look back in the passage for a mention of lion tricks.

6. **Why should you thank Henri Martin if you like circus animal acts?**

   A Martin thought of the idea for the first circus.

   B Martin presented many circus shows in Paris, France.

   C Martin was the first trainer to use animals in a circus act.

   D Martin trained his animals and made sure they feared

HELPFUL HINT
This question asks you to draw a conclusion. What did Henri Martin do that had to do with circus animal acts?

FOR THE OPEN-ENDED QUESTION BELOW, REMEMBER TO:
- Pay attention to what the question is asking you.
- Be sure to answer everything the question asks you.
- Fully explain what you mean by your answer.
- Use details from the passage.

7. **You have just read the passage "Animal Acts." What do you think about animals performing in circuses? Do you think this a good thing for wild animals to be doing? Explain your answer.**

_____

_____

_____

_____

_____

_____

_____

_____

_____

_____

_____

_____

_____

_____

YOU TRY IT

Betsy's Birthday Pony

Betsy has a love affair with horses. She reads every book she can about them. She even started collecting carousel horse figures. You can guess what she wants for her next birthday— a real live pony.

"Betsy, we know that you would like a pony of your very own," her father says. "Your mother and I know that a pony is expensive and requires a lot of care."

"We've talked with people who own ponies and to people who run boarding stables. Let your father tell you some of the things we've learned," her mother said.

Betsy's shoulders slumped. Her dream of owning a pony was not to be.

"We've learned Shetland or Dartmoor ponies are good for children. Either one would cost a lot of money. But it's the costs after that that concern us," her father said.

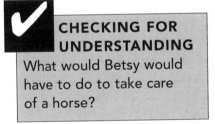

CHECKING FOR UNDERSTANDING
What would Betsy would have to do to take care of a horse?

"Let's start with what you would need to wear," her mother put in.

"But Mom, I don't need those fancy jackets and riding pants," Betsy assures her. "I wouldn't need them until I was a very good rider in a horse show."

"We know that," her father replies, "but you still need gloves, good boots, and a special hat. We can't have you falling off and hitting your head."

Betsy wants to say that she won't fall off but, of course, that could happen.

"Since we don't own a farm, a pony has to be kept at a stable. It will need shots every year. Horses get some of the same illnesses we do. Then, it will need oral medicine every two months."

"I didn't know that," Betsy says in wonder.

"The pony's feet need care. Stones get into their feet and so do infections. Ponies need shoes. These may need to be replaced every six to eight weeks," her father tells her.

Her mother adds, "Every day a pony needs care. It needs plenty of food and water. It also needs mineral salt blocks".

"I think maybe it is most important," her mother suggests, "that a rider and a horse need to bond. They both have to come to trust each other. That means lots of brushing of the pony's coat, and hugs and nuzzles. These things can't be done just once in a while."

"I know you would want to do these things. All the stables are just too far away. Your mother or I would have to drive you there. So, you couldn't be there every day," her dad explains.

"We do have a solution," her mother says cheerfully.

Betsy perks up, waiting to hear more.

18 "Yes, we think that we can 'give you a pony' without your owning one. Your mother has agreed to take you once a week to ride a pony. We spoke with Mr. Graham, a stable owner. He says that you can take riding lessons. Each week, you will have the same pony. So, you can think of it as your very own pony. How does that sound to you?"

"Oh, Dad, that's great! I love it! How soon can I start?"

"Would tomorrow be too soon?" he says with a chuckle.

Betsy rushes first to one parent and then to the other, hugging and kissing them. Her joy tells how she feels. Betsy does get a pony for her birthday after all. ■

1. **How do Betsy's parents know what is involved in owning a pony?**

   A They have read many books about horses.

   B They have owned a lot of tiny horse figurines.

   C They have talked with someone who owns a pony.

   D They owned a pony when they lived on a farm.

   ★ HELPFUL HINT
   This question asks you to recall information stated during the story. If you are unsure of the answer, reread the passage. You should look for any mention of what having a pony involves.

2. **Which suffix can you add to "need" to make it mean "not needed"?**

   A -less

   B -ness

   C -ful

   D -ing

   ★ HELPFUL HINT
   This question asks you to look at the parts of words. You should add each possible answer to the end of the word "need" and try to find which one makes it mean "not needed."

3. **What is the *most* important piece of clothing a rider should wear?**

   A a fancy jacket

   B a special hat

   C a pair of boots

   D a pair of gloves

   ★ HELPFUL HINT
   This question asks you to draw a conclusion. If you were going to ride a horse, what do you think would be the most important thing to wear?

4. How are people and horses alike?

  A Both eat the same foods.

  B Both live inside stables.

  C Both get the same kinds of illnesses.

  D Both must have their coats brushed.

HELPFUL HINT

This question also asks you to draw a conclusion. Where in the story did it mention anything about horses that could also relate to people? If you're unsure, go back and reread the passage.

5. Why can't Betsy go to the stable every day?

  A Betsy can't miss her classes.

  B Betsy has too many chores to do.

  C The stables aren't open every day.

  D The stables are very far away.

HELPFUL HINT

This question asks you to recall information stated during the story. If you are unsure of the answer, reread the passage. You should look for any mention of Betsy going to the stable.

6. What does the word "agreed" mean in paragraph 18?

  A moved

  B allowed

  C helped

  D played

HELPFUL HINT

This question asks you to select the meaning of the word "agreed." Are there any clues in the other sentences in paragraph 18 to let you know the word's meaning?

FOR THE OPEN-ENDED QUESTION BELOW, REMEMBER TO:
• Pay attention to what the question is asking you.
• Be sure to answer everything the question asks you.
• Fully explain what you mean by your answer.
• Use details from the story.

7. **Do you think that Betsy's parents made a good decision about her birthday present? Explain your answer.**

_____

_____

_____

_____

_____

_____

_____

_____

_____

_____

_____

_____

_____

Chapter 2: **Understanding Text**
Context Clues and Author's Purpose

When taking any test, it is always important to really think about what you are reading. If you make a habit of doing this, you will recognize a new word within the text right away. Then you can try to determine its meaning by studying the words around it, the **context clues**.

Thinking about what you are reading could also lead you to wonder why the author has written the text. What is the author trying to say? The **author's purpose** can provide a deeper understanding of the text's meaning. It can also give you a hint as to why the words you see may have been selected.

RL.3.4, RI.3.4, RF.3.3: RECOGNITION OF CONTEXT CLUES

You Try It

You have just finished reading a story. You saw a word that you are not familiar with. What do you do?

- Do you look the word up in a dictionary right away?

- Do you try to guess what the new word means by re-reading the paragraph?

When taking a test, you may not have the opportunity to use a dictionary to look up a new word. Your best bet is to use context clues to give you hints about the word's meaning.

What are context clues?

The words and sentences around a word are the **context**. A **clue** is something that helps solve a problem.

The sentences, phrases, and words that are surrounding a new word are **context clues**.

Finding the meaning of the new word is the challenge.

So, the context clues help you to find the meaning of the new word. Sometimes just reading the paragraph again and looking at the words around the new word will let you know what it means.

How do I use context clues?

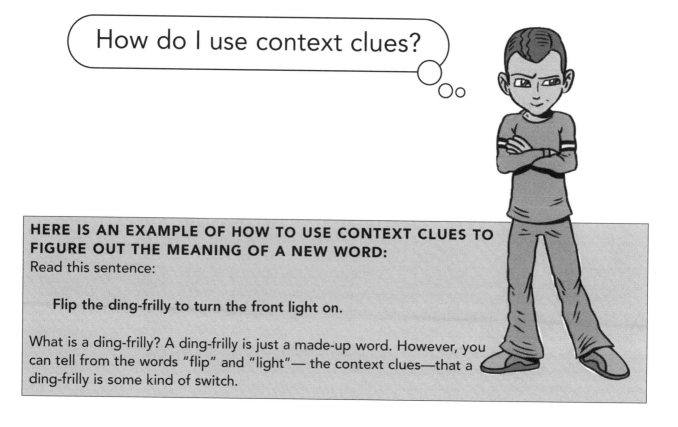

HERE IS AN EXAMPLE OF HOW TO USE CONTEXT CLUES TO FIGURE OUT THE MEANING OF A NEW WORD:

Read this sentence:

Flip the ding-frilly to turn the front light on.

What is a ding-frilly? A ding-frilly is just a made-up word. However, you can tell from the words "flip" and "light"— the context clues—that a ding-frilly is some kind of switch.

Context clues give hints about the meaning of a word.

HERE IS ANOTHER EXAMPLE:

"Before I get a frame, I have to measure the picture," Dad said. *"Please lend me your thingamajig."*

What is a thingamajig?

A thingamajig is a made-up word. However, you can tell from the words "measure" and "picture"—the context clues—that by thingamajig, Dad means a ruler of some kind.

Here's one for you to try:

Mr. Abari spoke softly to the students and said, "Please raise your left graxilflax if you know the answer."

What is a graxilflax? (Write your guesses below.)

_____

_____

Which words in the sentence gave you clues? (Write your guesses below.)

_____

_____

Could the same word have two meanings?

Sometimes when you are reading, you may not realize at first that you have come across a new word.

The word you see in the sentence may be a word that you think that you already know the meaning of.

However, when you reread the sentence, you might notice that the word meaning you know does not make sense in this sentence.

This could be the case if the word has **more than one meaning**. The same word could have even more than two meanings. It could mean many different things.

In these cases, it would be best for you to go to the dictionary to find out which meaning of the word is being used in that sentence.

When going to a dictionary is not option, as when taking a test, it is best to use the context clues in the sentence to determine what the word means.

HERE ARE SOME TIPS FOR DISCOVERING THE WORD'S MEANING:
• If you can, start with the definition that you already know.
• Is that the definition of the word as it is used in this sentence?
• If not, look at the sentence. What are the words around the new word?
• Do those words give you any clues about the word's meaning?

How can I tell which meaning is being used?

Here are some dictionary entries and sample sentences for some words with multiple meanings.

> **bow** [bou]
> (verb) 1. incline the head or body, as in greeting.
> (noun) 2. curved piece of wood, with a string stretched across its ends, for shooting arrows.
> (noun) 3. a ribbon tied in a decorative knot.

Example using definition 1: Please bow to the queen as she passes by.

Example using definition 2: The archer got his bow ready to shoot the arrows.

Example using definition 3: Mia untied the bow, eager to unwrap the gift.

> **watch** [wach]
> (verb) 1. to keep eyes fixed upon.
> (noun) 2. small portable timepiece for the wrist or pocket.

Example using definition 1: "John! Watch what you're doing!" Mother scolded.

Example using definition 2: The guard looked at his watch as the man walked by again.

LET'S TRY IT TOGETHER

DIRECTIONS: Read the story below and we'll discuss the questions together.

Rebecca and the Rockets

Rebecca waited for the soccer match to begin. She was ready to do her best for her team, the Rockets. She had practiced after school all week. If the Rockets won, they would advance to the semi-finals and face the Chargers.

Most of her teammates thought that the Chargers were the best team in the league, but Rebecca didn't think so. As the referee walked onto the field to start the game, Rebecca had a big smile on her face. She knew the Chargers were no match for the Rockets. ■

If the same word appears in two sentences, how do I know if they both have the same meaning?

It's best to use context clues to figure out what new words mean.

What does the word "match" mean in this sentence?

Rebecca waited for the soccer **match** to begin.

Let's look at the words around "match". In this sentence the word *soccer* is describing the word *match*. That would mean that the *match* in this sentence means soccer "game or contest."

How can I figure out what words mean?

What does the word "match" mean in this sentence?

> She knew the Chargers were no **match** for the Rockets.

Does the word "match" mean the same thing in this sentence as it did in the first one? No, it doesn't. This is an example of a word having more than one meaning.

In this sentence, the word "match" is talking about the Chargers versus the Rockets. It is saying that the Chargers are no "match" for Rebecca's team. This would mean that in this sentence, "match" means "equal to," or "an equal competitor."

What does the word "advance" mean in this sentence?

> If the Rockets won, they would **advance** to the semi-finals and face the Chargers.

In this sentence the word "advance" is talking about what would happen if the team won. The next step for the team would be to "advance" to the semi-finals.

Most of the time when you think of taking steps, you are moving forward. Knowing that, you could guess that in this sentence "advance" means "to go on, or move forward."

> If the Rockets won, they would advance to the semi-finals and **face** the Chargers.

When you think of the word "face", the first definition that probably comes to mind is the part of the body with eyes, nose, and mouth. However, based on the context clues in this sentence, it's clear that is not the definition meant in this sentence.

We already know that "advance" means "to go on." If the Rockets won, they would go on to the semi-finals. You could guess that they would play against another team in the semi-finals.

Knowing that, you could then further guess that the team the Rockets would play would be the Chargers. Therefore, in this sentence, "face" could mean "to be opposite, challenge."

What does the word "face" mean in this sentence?

> As the referee walked onto the field to start the game, Rebecca had a big smile on her **face**.

Reading this sentence, you can tell that the definition of "face" from the sentence at the top of the page is not the same one being used here.

The sentence says that Rebecca has a big smile. Think about where on your body your smile is. It's on your face!

So now you can tell that "face" means the part of your body, "the front of the head, from forehead to chin."

RL3.10, RF.3.10: READ AND COMPREHEND

During an average school day, you probably do a lot of reading.

You may read from a history textbook, a novel, a math workbook, or even a letter from your teacher. While all of these may have different styles of writing, they have one thing in common—they were written with a purpose.

What is an author's purpose for writing?

An **author's purpose** is the reason, or goal, an author has for writing something.

Everything you read is written by an author. Whether it is part of a history textbook, a novel, a math workbook, or even a letter form your teacher. Each of these is written by an author.

Each author has a **purpose**; or reason, for writing what he or she has written. Take a look at the chart below for some common purpose for writing.

AUTHOR'S PURPOSE FOR WRITING

Examples of Types of Writing	Author's Purpose
fictional story about a monkey in space	to entertain the reader
an informational passage about the water cycle	to teach the reader
a personal story about the riding a bike for the first time	to share a personal story

YOU TRY IT

> **DIRECTIONS:** Read the story below and we'll discuss the questions together.

Dena's New Puppy

Dena quickly tightened her grip on Murphy's leash as she saw the birds gathered in the park. After two weeks, she had quickly learned her new puppy's traits and knew that, if he had the chance, he would try to chase after the birds.

Normally she might have let him have his fun, but today she was exhausted. The early mornings were starting to wear on her. Each morning Murphy jumped on her bed and licked her face at sunrise. Dena liked to sleep in, but she now realized she wouldn't get to do that anytime soon.

After the morning wake-up call, Dena had to walk the dog and feed him. Then she usually had to clean up any mess he had made during the night, which was almost always. This all had to be done in time to catch the bus to school.

It was a lot of work, but Dena was determined. Her parents had been unsure about getting a puppy. They had thought it would be too much work. Dena wanted to show them that she could take on the new responsibility. It didn't hurt that Murphy always made her smile, no matter how early it was. ■

What was the author's purpose for writing this story?

Was it to persuade readers to get a puppy?

No, that is not the author's purpose in this story.
The author does not try to convince readers that they should have puppies of their own.

Was it to teach readers how to take care of a puppy?

No, that is also not the author's purpose in the story. The story does have information about taking care of a puppy, but the story is not teaching readers how to do it themselves.

Was it to entertain readers with a story about a girl and her puppy?

Yes, that is the author's purpose. The story is about Dena and her dog, and tells about their time together in an entertaining way.

When you are reading, ask yourself why the author has written what you are reading. If you remember to ask yourself several times while reading the passage, the hints about the author's purpose may be easier to see.

A **reader's purpose** is the reason why a reader reads something.

Just like authors have a purpose for writing, readers also have a purpose, or goal, for reading. You might read a comic strip or silly story to be entertained. You might read an encyclopedia or dictionary entry to learn something new about a topic.

As readers, we must set a purpose, or reason, to read something before we read it.

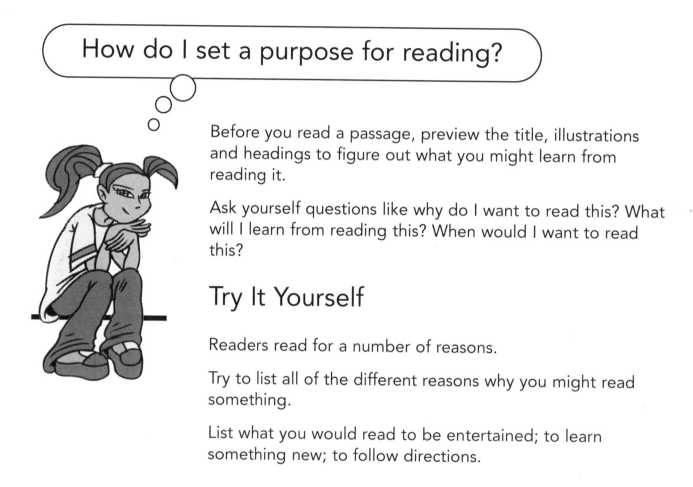

How do I set a purpose for reading?

Before you read a passage, preview the title, illustrations and headings to figure out what you might learn from reading it.

Ask yourself questions like why do I want to read this? What will I learn from reading this? When would I want to read this?

Try It Yourself

Readers read for a number of reasons.

Try to list all of the different reasons why you might read something.

List what you would read to be entertained; to learn something new; to follow directions.

_____

_____

_____

YOU TRY IT

Robert-Houdin: The First Modern Magician

Jean Robert-Houdin's father ran a small clock-making shop in Blois, France. When he was born in 1805, Jean was named Jean Eugene Robert. He added "Houdin" to his name later in life.

As a child, Jean was very interested in mechanical things. He loved to make automata. Automata were complex machines that showed different scenes. One of his early automata had a tiny rabbit that ran across a field. A hunter and his dog chased the rabbit. When the hunter's rifle fired, the rabbit disappeared. People loved to come to the clock store to see Jean's automata.

Poster for a Robert-Houdin magic show.

 CHECKING FOR UNDERSTANDING
Why do you think the writer decided to include what Jean liked to do as a young boy?

In spite of Jean's mechanical ability, his father wanted him to become a lawyer. At 18, he apprenticed Jean to a local lawyer, despite Jean's objections. Each morning Jean continued to build automata in his father's shop. Eventually, Jean's father realized his son would not be a lawyer.

His father allowed him to return to the family business. Jean made beautiful watches and continued designing automata in his spare time. In a short time, his skill became well known. People far and wide came to Jean's small French village to see his creations.

During this time, the magic bug bit Jean. He tried to visit every magic show he could. One day, he purchased a book on magic from a bookstore by mistake. It described how to perform magic tricks. Jean loved reading about how to do the tricks. He realized that magic would become his occupation. In a short time, he had learned sleight-of-hand magic tricks. These are tricks that involve using the hands to make things seem to appear and disappear from the magician's hands.

Soon Jean began to spend his evenings in a theater group. Through the group, he met and married his first wife, Josephe Houdin. Josephe's father was also a skilled watchmaker. He asked Jean to work with him in Paris. Jean added "Houdin" to his name and became known as Jean Eugene Robert-Houdin. Sadly, his wife died suddenly, leaving Jean with three small children.

Later, Jean remarried. His new wife, Marguerite Bracconier, suggested he put his automata in shows. With Marguerite's prompting, Jean entered one of his automata in a national exhibition. People loved his machine. Many asked him to make one for them. Now, Jean spent his time making automata for customers.

8 In spite of his success, Jean still wanted to be a magician. His wife prompted him to start his own magic show. At first, Houdin was not sure he could be a successful magician. His ideas about magic shows were very different from those of other magicians at the time.

He wanted his automata to be the main attraction in his show. The regular magic tricks would be performed between the automata acts. He had unusual ideas about the stage set and what magicians should wear as well. He wanted his stage to be simple with few props and assistants. He felt that this would make his shows more mysterious.

Unlike other magicians of his day who dressed in robes, Houdin dressed in formal clothes. Houdin rebuilt the second floor of a building in Paris for his theater. He sold one of his automata to P.T. Barnum to pay for the building's remodeling. Houdin became the first magician to perform in a theater.

Soon Houdin was ready to put on his first show. He invited everyone he knew. Unfortunately, in spite of all his preparation, the first show was a disaster. Houdin was nervous and spoke in a monotone voice. Few people came to the show the following month. However, as his confidence grew, Jean became a better performer. People loved his shows. Soon the theater was full each night.

The centerpiece of his shows was his automata. One of his best machines was the "Orange Tree." It bloomed on stage as if by magic and seemed to grow oranges. Houdin then threw the oranges into the audience.

Houdin continued to perform in his theater. As his fame grew, he also toured Europe. Almost every show he held was sold out. Kings and queens also asked him to perform for them. Houdin was the most famous magician of his time.

In 1852, Houdin retired at the height of his fame. He gave his theater and show to his brother-in-law. Then, he retired to an estate in France. Here Houdin spent his time working on clocks powered by electricity. Many people thought he was crazy. Electricity was new and not that popular at the time. Over the years, Houdin continued to experiment with electricity. He made many things that were run with electricity. Once again, Jean Robert-Houdin was ahead of his time. The great magician died in 1871 at the age of 65. ∎

The twentieth-century magician Harry Houdini admired Robert-Houdin so much that he adopted Houdin's name for his own use.

1. **One purpose of the first paragraph is to**

   A describe the machines Jean made.

   B tell what Jean wanted to be.

   C show where Jean met his wife.

   D report where Jean was born.

⭐ **HELPFUL HINT**
This question asks you to think about The reason why the first paragraph was written and its placement within the passage. What information were you told about first?

2. **Why did people like coming to the clock-making shop?**

   A to have their watches fixed

   B to talk with Jean's father

   C to see Jean's automata

   D to buy gifts for their friends

⭐ **HELPFUL HINT**
This question asks you to remember a detail from the passage. Think back to where the passage mentioned the clock-making shop. If you're not sure of the answer, reread the second paragraph.

3. **"During this time, the magic bug bit Jean" means that**

   A Jean was bitten by a real bug.

   B Jean had no time to practice magic.

   C Jean became interested in magic.

   D Jean was becoming very sick.

⭐ **HELPFUL HINT**
This question asks you to predict what the author means by this statement. Reread the sentence and the paragraph it is in. Based on the Context clues, what is the author trying to say?

4. How were Jean and other magicians alike?

A All of them dressed in robes.

B All of them used automata.

C All of them performed tricks.

D All of them had many props.

HELPFUL HINT
This question asks you to draw a conclusion. The passage mentioned why Jean was different from other magicians. In order to answer this question, you may need to first recall what Jean did differently.

5. What does the word "success" mean in paragraph 8?

A happiness

B accomplishment

C misfortune

D feeling

HELPFUL HINT
This question asks you to select the meaning of the word "success." Are there any clues in the other sentences in paragraph eight to let you know the word's meaning?

6. What did Jean throw at the audience?

A coins

B papers

C oranges

D bird

HELPFUL HINT
This question asks you about a detail from the passage. If you are unsure of the answer, reread the section that describes this trick. Be sure to look for a mention of Jean performing.

FOR THE OPEN-ENDED QUESTION BELOW, REMEMBER TO:
• Pay attention to what the question is asking you.
• Be sure to answer everything the question asks you.
• Fully explain what you mean by your answer.
• Use details from the passage.

7. Explain how Jean Robert-Houdin was a person ahead of his time. Use information from the passage to support your answer.

_____

_____

_____

_____

_____

_____

_____

_____

_____

_____

_____

_____

_____

_____

_____

YOU TRY IT

DIRECTIONS: Read this passage, and answer the questions that follow.

Is It Spring Yet?

Some people see the first robin or early flowers as signals of spring. For others, February 2nd signals spring. This day forecasts what's to come. It's known as Groundhog Day.

CHECKING FOR UNDERSTANDING

What are some things that you may identify as signals that spring is coming?

People wait for the groundhog to appear to tell if spring is soon to arrive. That depends on whether or not the groundhog sees its shadow. If it sees its shadow, there will be six more weeks of winter. If it doesn't, it means an early spring.

At least, that is how the story goes. There are several interesting things both about the groundhog and Groundhog Day.

Let's look first at the groundhog and the animal groups to which it belongs. An animal classification shows that the groundhog is part of one family of rodents.

ANIMAL CLASSIFICATION

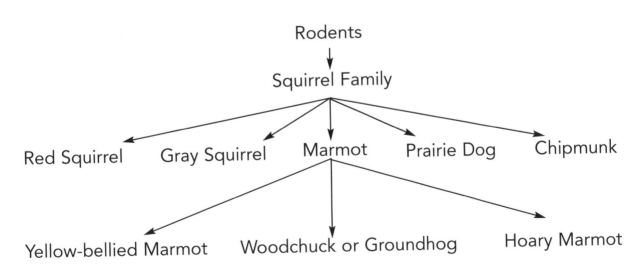

5   Groundhogs, or woodchucks, are timid animals. They grow to be up to two feet in length. Their front feet each have four toes. This lets them grasp food as a human hand does. They eat clover, alfalfa, and some grasses. They live in burrows with three exits—a front, a back, and a drop hole. The drop hole goes down more than two feet into the ground. This lets woodchucks escape from their enemies.

Groundhogs are black or brown bushy-tailed animals. They hibernate from December to March. By February, they're about to wake up. That helps explain their role in Groundhog Day.

Groundhog Day Facts

February 2nd was picked as Groundhog Day for a special reason. It is halfway between the fall and spring dates when the days and nights are twelve hours long.

February is the cloudiest month across the United States. So, the woodchuck is not likely to see its shadow. That means an early spring! ■

1. **What is this passage *mostly* about?**

    A   sorting the different kinds of rodents

    B   signs of spring in the woods and fields

    C   springtime and groundhogs

    D   what a groundhog burrow is like

HELPFUL HINT

This question asks you to think about what this passage is really about. What do you think the author was trying to do when he or she wrote this passage?

2. **What does it mean if a groundhog sees its shadow on February 2nd?**

    A   The sun will shine brighter.

    B   The wind will blow harder.

    C   Spring will come early.

    D   Winter will last longer.

HELPFUL HINT

This question asks you about a detail from the passage. If you are unsure of the answer, reread the second paragraph. Look for the place where the passage tells you about the groundhog seeing its shadow.

3. **Why does the author *most likely* include the animal classification key?**

    A   to tell readers why groundhogs are very important to the weather

    B   to show readers which animal family the groundhog belongs to

    C   to show readers where most groundhogs are found in the spring

    D   to tell readers how groundhogs are different from other animals

HELPFUL HINT

This question asks you to think about the reason why the author decided to include a key about groundhogs. Did the key help you to understand anything more about groundhogs?

4. What does the word "grasp" mean in paragraph 5?

A push

B take

C bite

D hold

HELPFUL HINT
This question asks you to select the meaning of the word "grasp." Are there any clues in the other sentences in paragraph five to let you know the word's meaning?

5. What do *most* groundhogs do in February?

A search for food

B make a burrow

C run away

D wake up

HELPFUL HINT
This question asks you about a detail from the passage. Do you remember what it said about what groundhogs do in February? If you are unsure of the answer, reread the last few paragraphs.

6. It is likely that the groundhog won't see its shadow on Groundhog Day because

A February is the cloudiest month.

B February is the coldest month.

C the groundhog will stay inside its burrow.

D the groundhog will be looking for food.

HELPFUL HINT
This question asks you to recall information stated during the passage. If you are unsure of the answer, reread the end of the passage. You should look for any mention of the groundhog seeing its shadow.

FOR THE OPEN-ENDED QUESTION BELOW, REMEMBER TO:
- Pay attention to what the question is asking you.
- Be sure to answer everything the question asks you.
- Fully explain what you mean by your answer.
- Use details from the passage.

7. **What were some facts that you learned from this passage about the groundhog? Write as many as you can. Be sure to write at least three.**

_____

_____

_____

_____

_____

_____

_____

_____

_____

_____

_____

_____

YOU TRY IT

Become a Puppeteer

Become a puppeteer. Make your friends laugh with puppets you make. Everyone can do it. All you need to do is to follow the steps in this pamphlet. You and your friends should get a grown-up to help you with this project.

Step 1 — Make up a story.

The first thing you will need to do is to decide which story you will tell. Get a few of your friends and talk about funny things that have happened. Choose a topic that can be shown with puppets.

CHECKING FOR UNDERSTANDING
Why would it be important to plan out the story you want to tell in advance?

Talk through the story. Identify the puppets you will need to tell the story. For your first puppet show, keep the story line simple. Use only a few puppets to tell the story. Once you know the general story and have decided which puppets you will need, move to step 2.

Step 2 — Make the puppets for your show.

There are many different types of puppets. For your first show, though, it is better to use finger puppets. These are the easiest puppets to make and to use. They require sheets of paper, thin cardboard, glue, and tape. You will also need crayons and magic markers.

Cut a three-inch-wide strip of paper long enough to wrap around your finger. Wrap it around your finger and tape the ends. The tube should fit loosely on your finger. Then, cut a circle from a piece of thin cardboard. Make a face on the circle. This can be done using crayons or pieces of paper. Glue or tape the face to the tube. Finally, cut tissue paper into strips. Put these strips around the face for hair.

You should design the faces of your puppets before you make any drawings. Doing this allows you to see if the faces you are making are really what you want for the puppets. 6

Step 3 — Practice with your finger puppets.

Retell the story you and your friends will act out using your puppets. Remember to have the puppets face the characters they are talking to. Decide which props, if any, you will need for your story. Go over the story until you are sure of what the puppets will say and how they will act.

Step 4 — Build a theater.

In this step you will make the box behind which the people with the puppets kneel or stand. You will need one or more large cardboard boxes, packing tape, and paint. An appliance box is best for making a theater. The box needs to be large enough so that the puppeteers can kneel or stand behind it and not be seen by the audience.

Cut off the top of the box, leaving a five-inch edge. This edge will become the ledge where you will place any props that you use in your show. Next, cut one side off the box so you will be able to enter it without being seen. Tape the sides together so the box will stand without falling over. Finally, paint and decorate the box.

Step 5 — Present your show.

You should rehearse your show several times before you present it to your friends and family. Have a friend watch you give the show. He or she will be able to tell you how the show looks to the audience.

Remember, when presenting your show:

- Have the puppets face outward toward the audience.

- Vary the pace of the show. This keeps it exciting for the audience.

- Give the puppets unique looks and personalities. This helps to make their actions more real.

- Invite your friends and give your puppet show.

There are other types of puppets you could use when putting on a show. A sampling of other types of puppets includes: glove, rod, shadow, and string puppets. There are books in your library that tell you how to make these and many more types of puppets. ■

1. **What type of story is <u>best</u> for a puppet show?**

A a sad story

B an adventure story

C a funny story

D a scary story

HELPFUL HINT

This question asks you about a detail rom the passage. Think about what the passage said about picking a story for a puppet show. If you are unsure of the answer, reread the Step 1.

2. **What is the second step to becoming a puppeteer?**

A making up a story for a show

B making puppets for the show

C practicing with your puppets

D presenting the show you made up

HELPFUL HINT

This question asks you to select the meaning of the word "design." Are there any clues in the other sentences in the sixth paragraph to help you know the word's meaning?

3. **What does the word "design" mean in the sixth paragraph?**

A change

B hide

C see

D sketch

HELPFUL HINT

This question asks you to think about the reason why the author decided to include bullet points in step five. Did the bullet points help you as a reader? How did they do that?

4. In step five, the author uses bullets to

  A put things in the order of how important they are.

  B tell what the audience should do during the show.

  C remind you to invite friends to the puppet show.

  D help readers to remember four important things.

HELPFUL HINT
This question asks you to think about the reason why the author decided to include bullet points in step five. Did the bullet points help you as a reader? How did they do that?

5. In which task is it probably *most* important to have a grownup's help?

  A when cutting the top off the box

  B when taping the sides of the box

  C when wrapping paper around your finger

  D when making a face on the circle

HELPFUL HINT
This question asks you to make a judgment about a part of the passage. Think about what you would do to complete each of steps. Is there anything that you would ask a grownup to help you with?

6. The purpose of the last paragraph is to

  A give ideas to keep the show entertaining.

  B give more ideas about making a play.

  C talk about other kinds of puppets.

  D tell about a trip to the local library.

HELPFUL HINT
This question asks you to think about why the author wrote the last paragraph. Reread the paragraph. Why do you think the author decided to include this paragraph in the passage?

FOR THE OPEN-ENDED QUESTION BELOW, REMEMBER TO:
- Pay attention to what the question is asking you.
- Be sure to answer everything the question asks you.
- Fully explain what you mean by your answer.
- Use details from the passage.

7. String puppets are puppets that have strings attached to their bodies. You can control their movements by pulling on their strings.

   - Explain why string puppets would *most likely* be harder to make and use than finger puppets.

   - Use what you learned about finger puppets to help you in your response.

YOU TRY IT

DIRECTIONS: Read this passage, and answer the questions that follow.

Ponies

Horses can be found all over the world. There are many different types of horses. One of them is the pony. A pony can be classified as a pony by its height. Ponies, like horses, are measured using the term "hands." A hand is four inches.

A pony is under 14.2 hands, or 56.8 inches, high. The measure is taken from the ground to the horse's withers. The withers is the point high on the horse's shoulder. It is between the neck and the back. There is one pony that is not measured in hands. That is the Shetland pony, which may measure up to forty inches high.

Some well-known ponies had their beginnings in different countries. Let's take a look at some of them. We'll begin with the famous Shetland ponies.

Shetland

The Shetland Islands are northeast of the United Kingdom. It is a very cold region. This pony is a small breed. Its thick coat gives protection from the cold. This pony is very intelligent and has a long life.

It is a good riding pony for children. It also was a pack animal. In 1850, some of them were brought to England. They were used to work in coal mines. Shetlands are beautiful, gentle animals.

Welsh and Welsh Cob

This pony comes from the Welsh mountain area. Wales is a section of the United Kingdom. It is southwest of England.

The Welsh pony, like the Shetland, was used to work in the coal mines. It is a very hardy and durable animal. The Welsh Cob is a pony known for its high-stepping gait. This ability is valued in a show horse.

The Welsh pony was crossed with the Hackney horse. It produced the Hackney show pony. This pony is from forty-six to fifty-six inches high.

Connemara

Connemara is a section of Ireland. This animal is fifty-four to sixty inches tall. It comes in most colors. This is a gentle pony. It is both hardy and sure-footed. This Connemara is known as a jumper and a show pony.

Dartmoor

England has nine native-type horses. One is the Dartmoor. It is about twelve hands high. Like some others, it is a good children's pony. Its colors are brown, black, or bay. ("Bay" describes a horse with a brown body and black mane and tail.)

CHECKING FOR UNDERSTANDING
Why would the author put quotation marks around a word?

American

In 1950, an American pony was noted. The Nez Perce tribe had a good riding horse called the Appaloosa. This horse had a mottled coat. It also had striped hooves. The American pony was the result of the crossbreeding of this horse with the Shetland pony. ∎

1. **What is this passage *mostly* about?**

    A   how to take care of a pony

    B   how ponies and horses are different

    C   the many different kinds of ponies

    D   the places ponies are used

HELPFUL HINT
This question asks you to think about the central idea of the passage. If you are unsure of the answer, skim the passage. What is the passage trying to tell you?

2. **The purpose of the first paragraph is to**

    A   tell readers how to tell if a horse is a pony.

    B   show readers how most ponies will act.

    C   tell readers where most ponies come from.

    D   show readers what most ponies look like.

HELPFUL HINT
This question asks you to think about why the author wrote the first paragraph. Reread the paragraph. Why do you think the author decided to include this paragraph in the passage?

3. **How are the Shetland and Welsh ponies alike?**

    A   Both came from the island of Wales.

    B   Both have very thick coats.

    C   Both are good riding ponies for kids.

    D   Both were used in coal mines.

HELPFUL HINT
This question asks you to draw a conclusion. The passage talked about both Shetland and Welsh ponies. Was there anything that was similar between the two?

4. Where is the Connemara pony from?

   A   England

   B   Ireland

   C   America

   D   Wales

HELPFUL HINT

This question asks you about a detail from the passage. Think about what the passage said about the Connemara pony. If you are unsure of the answer, reread that section.

5. Which is used to measure a pony's height?

   A   inches

   B   feet

   C   hands

   D   miles

HELPFUL HINT

This question asks you about a detail from the passage. Think about what the passage said about measuring a pony's height. If you are unsure of the answer, reread the first two paragraphs.

6. Which horse comes in a bay color?

   A   Connemara

   B   Shetland

   C   American

   D   Dartmoor

HELPFUL HINT

This question asks you about a detail from the passage. If you are unsure of the answer, skim the passage, looking for a mention of a pony being a bay color.

FOR THE OPEN-ENDED QUESTION BELOW, REMEMBER TO:
- Pay attention to what the question is asking you.
- Be sure to answer everything the question asks you.
- Fully explain what you mean by your answer.
- Use details from the passage.

7. **Why would a pony be a good choice as the first horse for young children to learn to ride? Use your own thoughts and explain your answer.**

_____

_____

_____

_____

_____

_____

_____

_____

_____

_____

_____

_____

_____

YOU TRY IT

DIRECTIONS: Read this passage and answer the questions that follow.

INTRODUCTION: This passage tells about rodeo clowns and the special role they play during the bull-riding events.

Rodeo Clowns

Clowns have been a part of rodeos for a long time. However, over the years, what they do at a rodeo has changed. In the beginning, clowns did their acts between events. They helped to make the time pass for the people in the stands.

Now the main job of most rodeo clowns is to protect the bull riders from serious injury or death. Each time a cowboy rides a bull into the ring, there are clowns in the ring. The clowns' job is to distract the bull when a cowboy falls. Most of the time, they can do this safely. Protecting the cowboy is not easy, though.

 CHECKING FOR UNDERSTANDING

What are some reasons why a bull is considered more dangerous than a horse?

A bull, unlike a horse, will charge anything that moves. Horses will not usually charge or step on a person. Bulls, however, will run directly through a person when charging. Bulls are fast and agile. They can also change direction suddenly. This makes bulls very dangerous in the ring.

If you have ever been to a rodeo, you may know that there are three types of rodeo clowns. Each type serves has a role in the rodeo show. It is not unusual for a clown to play more than one part during a rodeo.

The bullfighting clowns distract the bull and help to get it back into its pen. These clowns stand directly in front of the bull when the rider gets off. Clowns want the bull to chase them. They may even swat at the bull to get its attention.

The barrel clown hides in a barrel in the ring. This barrel is always in the ring during bull-riding events. It serves two purposes. First, it is a safe place for the cowboy to hide after he gets off the bull. The barrel is also a large target. When it is moved, it gets the bull's attention.

The bull usually will charge the barrel. When the bull hits the barrel, it just rolls away from his charge. The barrel clown stays in the barrel and rolls it away from the bull's charge.

Comedy clowns are the third type of rodeo clown. Their job is to entertain the people in the stands. They usually do not go into a ring with animals.

Rodeo clowns in the ring with the bulls do wear protective equipment. They have special vests and hip pads. They will also wear pads on their legs and ankles. While these do help, most clowns still get hurt during their careers.

One rodeo clown suffered 24 broken bones in a 25-year career. He also had three concussions and injured his ear. This clown felt that getting hit by a bull was like being hit by a car going 20 miles per hour. He said, "It is not IF you are going to get hurt. It's WHEN and how badly." He even had an 1,800-pound bull land on top of him. Amazingly, he walked away without a scratch. This rodeo clown was very lucky.

 10

Rodeo clowns spend time looking at the bulls in the pens before the rodeo starts. They try to notice how each bull behaves. This often helps the clowns avoid getting hurt by certain bulls.

All rodeo clowns paint their faces like other clowns. They also wear funny-looking clothing and wigs. Most, however, do not wear big shoes. The clowns that distract bulls do not wear big floppy shoes. They need to be able to run away. Comedy clowns may wear big floppy shoes. However, they are not usually in the ring with the animals.

The sponsor of the rodeo pays rodeo clowns. They may also get large companies to sponsor them. When this happens, the clowns advertise the products of that company.

Only a small group of rodeo clowns makes a full-time living by being clowns. Most do it as a part-time job. Popular clowns work between 130 and 190 days a year. Most clowns bring their own trailers with them. This is where they live and where they keep their props and clothes.

The next time you see rodeo clowns, remember that they play an important role. Most are there to protect the cowboys from the bulls. Without rodeo clowns in the ring, many bull riders would be hurt. ■

1. **What is this passage *mostly* about?**

   A   going to rodeo clown school

   B   the work of a rodeo clown

   C   how rodeo clowns have changed over the years

   D   ways to be safe when you visit a rodeo

   ⭐ **HELPFUL HINT**
   This question asks you to think about the main idea of the passage. If you are unsure of the answer, skim the passage. What is the passage trying to tell you

2. **What will clowns do to get a bull's attention?**

   A   swat at the bull

   B   wear big shoes

   C   throw a barrel

   D   look in the pens

   ⭐ **HELPFUL HINT**
   This question asks you about a detail from the passage. If you are unsure of the answer, skim the passage, looking for a mention of what the clowns do to distract bulls.

3. **What does the word "suffered" mean in paragraph 10?**

   A   ruined

   B   made fun

   C   experienced

   D   discovered

   ⭐ **HELPFUL HINT**
   This question asks you to select the meaning of the word "suffered." Are there any clues in the other sentences in the tenth paragraph to help you know the word's meaning?

4. What do rodeo clowns do before a rodeo?

   A entertain people in the stands

   B look at the bulls in the pens

   C feed and help the bull riders

   D hide inside barrels in the ring

HELPFUL HINT

This question asks you to recall what the passage said about the customary tasks of the rodeo clowns. If you are unsure of the answer, look back toward the end of the passage.

5. Which clown might wear big shoes?

   A a comedy clown

   B a barrel clown

   C a bullfighting clown

   D a sponsored clown

HELPFUL HINT

This question asks you about a detail from the passage. Can you imagine which of the clowns would wear big shoes? If you are unsure of the answer, reread the 12th paragraph.

6. Which is one kind of protective equipment rodeo clowns wear?

   A big shoes

   B funny hair

   C hip pads

   D barrels

HELPFUL HINT

This question asks you about a detail from the passage. If you are unsure of the answer, reread the ninth paragraph. You should look for the place where the author mentions protective equipment.

FOR THE OPEN-ENDED QUESTION BELOW, REMEMBER TO:
• Pay attention to what the question is asking you.
• Be sure to answer everything the question asks you.
• Fully explain what you mean by your answer.
• Use details from the passage.

7. **What kind of person would make a good rodeo clown? Use information from the passage to support your response.**

_____

_____

_____

_____

_____

_____

_____

_____

_____

_____

_____

_____

_____

_____

Chapter 3: **Analyzing Text**
Text Organization/Extrapolation
of Information

In this chapter we will learn about the genres of narrative writing and everyday text. You will read many different examples of each of these types of writing. We will also learn about why stories are told in a certain order. Finally, we will learn how to identify what the author is trying to say in each story.

RL.3.5, RI.3.5: RECOGNITION OF TEXT ORGANIZATION

You Try It

You have just finished reading a story. Your teacher asks you to identify the genre of the passage. How do you know which genre it is?

- Do you look at how the text is organized?

- Do you look at the style of the text?

Your best bet would be to look at both of the above. The topic of the passage may also help you to figure out the genre.

Each story has three important parts. No matter how short or long a story is, it has to have a **beginning**, a **middle**, and an **end**.

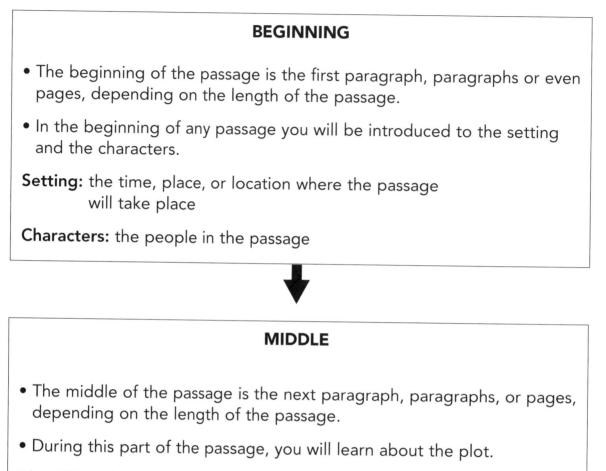

BEGINNING

- The beginning of the passage is the first paragraph, paragraphs or even pages, depending on the length of the passage.

- In the beginning of any passage you will be introduced to the setting and the characters.

Setting: the time, place, or location where the passage will take place

Characters: the people in the passage

MIDDLE

- The middle of the passage is the next paragraph, paragraphs, or pages, depending on the length of the passage.

- During this part of the passage, you will learn about the plot.

Plot: This is basically what the passage is about, the path the passage takes.

END

- The end of the passage is the final paragraph, paragraphs, or pages, depending on the length of the passage.

- The end of the passage contains the conclusion.

Conclusion: This is how the passage wraps up the plot; it explains how everything ends up.

What is a genre?

A **genre** is a category used to define a type of writing.

There are several different types of genres. You have probably read most of them already.

- The genres you will learn about in this chapter are **narrative text** and **everyday text.**

Some genres have sub-genres as well. A **sub-genre** can further explain what the story is about. Some sub-genres are science fiction, fantasy, and biography.

What is a narrative?

The first genre we will talk about is **narrative.**

Stories are narratives. They tell about a person, experience, or event, usually in the order in which the events took place.

Can you think of some of the many different kinds of stories?

Some examples are adventure stories, folk tales, fairy tales, and mystery stories.

- Many stories are made-up stories.
  These are **fiction**.

- Some stories are true or factual stories.
  These are **nonfiction**.

What is an everyday text?

An author writes an everyday text to tell the readers how to do something or to give them information that will be useful for their daily lives.

Often everyday texts have directions or steps. In order to understand an everyday text, you have to look at the way it is organized.

If it has steps, the steps are usually numbered (Step 1, Step 2…). There may be pictures to show how to do something.

If there are pictures, look carefully at each picture and pay attention to how the picture goes along with the text you are reading. You may have to answer questions about it.

Here is an example of an everyday text.

Yummy Fudgy Brownies	2 Eggs	1/4 cup Water	1/2 cup Vegetable Oil

Step 1	Preheat oven to 350 degrees.
Step 2	Stir brownie mix, eggs, water and vegetable oil in large bowl. Pour in pan.
Step 3	Bake for 35 minutes.

LET'S TRY IT TOGETHER

DIRECTIONS: Read the story below and we'll discuss the questions together.

Emily Meets Jacob

When she heard the front door open, Emily's head snapped up from her coloring book. "They're home!" she shouted as she jumped up from the table. Her grandmother smiled at her and stood up as well. The two of them walked out of the playroom and started toward the stairs. Grandma couldn't keep up with Emily as she rushed down the stairs and into her father's open arms.

"There's my girl," he said as he hugged her tight. Emily hugged him back just as tightly, happy to have them home. She looked up at her mother who was holding her new baby brother in a blanket.

"Good morning, Emmy," her mother said. Emily hugged her mother's leg and looked up at her smiling face. "Why don't you have a seat on the couch?" her mother suggested.

Emily rushed over to the couch in no time. "We know you're excited. Just be sure to stay still and be gentle with your brother," Grandma said. Emily nodded. "I'll be good," she said to her Grandma.

Her mother walked over to the couch and sat down next to her. "Emily, this is Jacob," she said gently as she placed the bundle into her arms.

"Nice to meet you, Jacob," Emily said, looking down at his tiny face. "I've been waiting to meet you for a while now. What took you so long?"

Emily's parents laughed. Grandma smiled. Even Jacob giggled. Emily smiled at all of them. What a great family I have, she thought to herself. ∎

What were the 3 parts of this story?

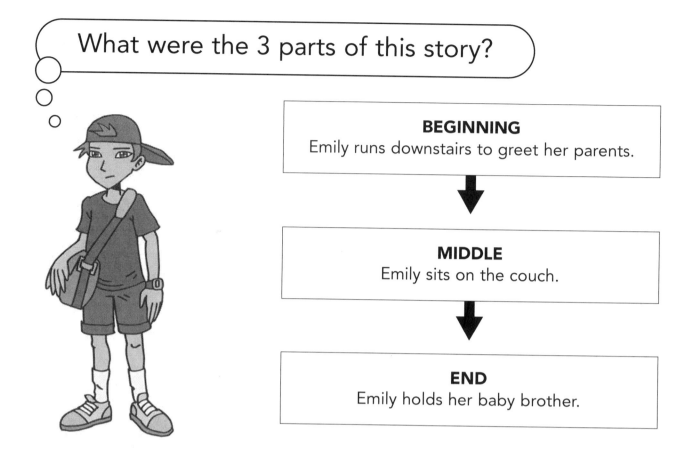

BEGINNING
Emily runs downstairs to greet her parents.

↓

MIDDLE
Emily sits on the couch.

↓

END
Emily holds her baby brother.

What genre is this story?

Is this story an example of everyday text?
No, this is not an example of everyday text. How do we know? We have learned that in everyday text, the author is trying to inform the reader about something. That is not the case in this story. Also, there are no steps or numbered points in this story.

Is this story an example of narrative text?
Yes, this story is an example of narrative text. How do we know? This story is about Emily's first meeting with her brother. It tells what happens in an organized way.

RL.3.10, RI.3.10: READ AND COMPREHEND

What is the author *really* trying to say?

Do the words you are reading always have to come right out and say what is happening?

Let's try to see how this works.

Directly Stated: When the author comes out and tells you everything you need to know in the story.

Not Directly Stated: When the author does not tell you everything you need to know. In these cases, you must figure out somethings for yourself.

You can get this meaning by thinking about what the words are telling you. Then ask yourself what the larger meaning might be.

What does the story tell you about life?

The **not-directly-stated** meaning may sometimes be the theme, or moral, of the story.

STORY SUMMARY:
Tim gets sick and needs help to catch up in school. His friend Julio visits every day after school and tells him all he needs to know about that day.

- The **directly-stated meaning** tells that Julio helps Tim when he gets sick.
- The moral of the story— **not-directly-stated** —is that good friends help one another no matter what.

YOU TRY IT

Jack in the Department Store

Jack walks past the same table of sweaters for the fourth time. He recognizes it because one of the sweaters is the same color his mom is wearing. But Jack can't find his mom. He got separated from her a few minutes ago during the shopping trip. His mother had always told him to stay close to her when they were shopping. Now Jack is completely lost and starting to get upset.

As Jack sees a flash of that same color again, he just keeps on walking, sure that it is just more of the sweaters. Suddenly Jack hears his mother's voice calling his name, he turns quickly in the direction of her voice. He sees the color of her sweater across the store, and he runs to her, relieved to have found her again. ∎

What is the *directly-stated* meaning of this story?

Is it that Jack's mother is wearing a sweater?
No, that is not the directly-stated meaning. Although the story mentions the sweater Jack's mother is wearing, that is just a detail. It does not tell us about the meaning of the story.

Is it that Jack is in a store with his mother?
No, that is not the directly-stated meaning either. A store is the setting of the story. Jack's mother is a character in the story.

Is it that Jack got separated from his mother?
Yes, that is the directly-stated meaning of the story. The words of the story let us know that Jack is lost in the store after he walked away from his mother.

What is the *not-directly-stated* meaning of this story?

Is it that Jack is walking around in circles?
No, that is not the not-directly-stated meaning. Although the author seems to want to show that Jack is walking around in circles because he passes the same table four times, that is not the implicit meaning of the story.

Is it that Jack's mother is looking for him?
No, that is not the not-directly-stated meaning either. You could guess that Jack's mother is looking for him, but that is not the implicit meaning of the story.

Is it that Jack should have listened to his mother and stayed close to her?
Yes, that is the not-directly-stated meaning of the story. Jack wandered off away from his mother in the story and ended up getting lost. His mother had warned him and now he knows he should have listened.

When you are reading, take note of the way the text is organized. It can tell you more about the kind of story you are reading.

Also, think about what the story is trying to tell you. Does the author have a deeper meaning than just what the words on the page are saying?

YOU TRY IT

DIRECTIONS:	Read this passage and answer the questions that follow.
INTRODUCTION:	This passage talks about how the modern circus was started and how it developed.

Modern Circus

The modern circus started in 1768 in England. Philip Astley owned a riding school. Each weekend he did tricks on the back of his horse. In the beginning, Astley did his tricks while riding straight past the crowd. Then, he found it easier to do his tricks while riding in a circle. He was the first to do horse tricks this way.

Doing tricks in a circle gave people more time to watch the trick. People loved it. In time, his show included clowns between the riding acts. The crowds got larger. Astley decided to construct a building for his shows.

The name, "circus," comes from Charles Hughes. He worked for Astley at his riding school. Hughes decided to start his own show in 1782. Hughes called his show "The Royal Circus." The word circus is Latin for "ring."

The circus came to America in 1793. It came first to Philadelphia. Later, it went to other cities. People loved it. Even George Washington came to see a show. The traveling circus had been born.

The early shows were simple. There were horse acts, music, and clowns. There might also have been a juggler and a rope dancer. By the 1850s, there would also be acrobats. The show was held in a field. Collections were taken up during the show. People gave what they wanted.

Later, the shows were done inside ropes. People had to pay to get into the show. The riding act was the main part of these shows. Each had a ringmaster, who would have the horses move in a circle. This allowed the rider to do his tricks. This is why the ringmasters wear riding clothes.

In the 1870s, large tents were added. A circus could now be set up anywhere. Weather was no longer a problem. About this time, the circus also expanded from one to three rings. Now there were more acts for people to watch. After the show, things were loaded into wagons. The wagons might take days to reach the next town.

The railroad brought changes to the circus. Now the circus could travel faster. It could also go to towns that had never before had a circus. The circus tents would be set up near the railroad track. The circus was a big event. Crowds came each night. After three days, the circus was gone. Only an open field showed where the circus had been.

Many small circuses were started in the 1800s. P.T. Barnum started one. The five Ringling brothers started another. In the 1900s, a few larger ones were formed. Many of the smaller circuses were combined. The Ringling Brothers and Barnum and Bailey Circus was the best known. It had more acts than any other circus.

Today, there are large and small circuses. The three large ones travel by train. They put on their shows in large buildings. The smaller circuses go to the smaller towns. They do their shows in fairgrounds and on ball fields. They may also put on shows in mall parking lots. The small

circuses travel in trucks, trailers, and motor homes.

Circus people may travel 20,000 miles a year. The smaller circuses may appear in over a hundred cities. The larger ones will appear in fewer cities. The larger circuses stay longer in one spot. Being in a circus is not an easy life. Most circus people, though, love it.

Much has changed since the first circus. There are more acts. There are also different types of acts. One thing is the same. People still come for the thrills and laughs. Everyone enjoys going to the circus. ■

1. **What was the circus able to do once it began to use ropes?**

   A do a set of shows in any weather

   B go from one ring to three rings

   C walk horses through a crowd

   D have people pay to see shows

HELPFUL HINT
This question asks you to recall information that you learned from reading the passage. If you are unsure of the answer, reread the passage. You should be looking for what happened after the circus added the ropes.

2. **What was in early circuses?**

   A horse acts

   B large tents

   C ringmasters

   D lion tamers

HELPFUL HINT
This question asks you to remember a detail from the passage. Can you recall what was the biggest factor in early circus shows? If you are unsure of the answer, reread the paragraphs that talk about the early shows.

3. **Circuses would *most likely* want more acts to**

   A use all the extra horses.

   B entertain more people.

   C keep the ringmaster busy.

   D open small new circuses.

HELPFUL HINT
This question asks you to make a guess based on what you have read. Why would circuses want to add more acts? What is one of the most important parts of a circus's success?

4. **How did railroads help circuses go to new towns?**

   A They brought bigger crowds to the circuses.

   B They let circuses set up near railroad tracks.

   C They took the circuses more places since they traveled faster.

   D They helped the circus to leave in three days.

HELPFUL HINT
This question asks you to make a guess about an outcome in the passage based on what you have read. What happened after the circuses started to travel on the railroad?

5. **Who first called a circus by that name?**

   A the Ringling brothers

   B Philip Astley

   C Charles Hughes

   D P.T. Barnum

HELPFUL HINT
This question asks you to remember a detail from the passage. If you are unsure about the answer, reread the early sections of the text. You should be looking for the the origin of the word "circus."

6. **Where do smaller circuses perform?**

   A railroad tracks

   B ball fields

   C large buildings

   D riding schools

HELPFUL HINT
This question asks you to remember a detail from the passage. If you are unsure about the answer, skim the passage. You should be looking for a mention of where the smaller circuses performed.

FOR THE OPEN-ENDED QUESTION BELOW, REMEMBER TO:
- Pay attention to what the question is asking you.
- Be sure to answer everything the question asks you.
- Fully explain what you mean by your answer.
- Use details from the passage.

7. If you were in charge of a circus, what problems do you think you would have in moving it from one place to another? List all the possible problems you can think of.

_____

_____

_____

_____

_____

_____

_____

_____

_____

_____

_____

_____

_____

YOU TRY IT

DIRECTIONS: Read this story, and answer the questions that follow.

Rabbit Run

The day is warm, just right for late spring. Grass has greened up and had its first few mowings. Rodney Rabbit is stretched out on his stomach beneath a lilac bush. Even without a breeze, he can smell the flowers above his head. It is the type of day he loves. He can do his favorite things— to be lazy and do nothing!

Rodney is a challenge for his mother. She has three young bunnies to care for. The other two are easy to handle. Midge, short for Midget, who is the smallest, stays close to home. Barney is brave, but alert to danger. That's not the way it is with Rodney!

Try as she might, Bertha Rabbit cannot get Rodney to understand that there are dangers about. For instance, a man with a big noisy machine travels all over the area. Behind him the grass and clover are left much shorter. If you want a good meal, you have to eat before you hear him coming. If you do, then you aren't hungry when you dash away to safety.

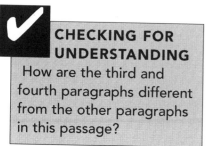

CHECKING FOR UNDERSTANDING
How are the third and fourth paragraphs different from the other paragraphs in this passage?

Bertha knows that there are other dangers, too. There is a large brown and white animal that comes romping around the lawn. It makes a loud barking noise. Bertha isn't sure if this animal means them harm. Maybe it just wants to play. She doesn't take any chances. When her nose picks up its scent or her large ears hear it coming, she warns her children.

Bertha has taught them two ways to avoid danger. One is to stay completely still. They are not to move their ears, twitch their whiskers, or blink their eyes. In this way the little rabbits can often escape detection. The other is to dash to their den

---

when Mother Rabbit thumps her hind foot. Midge and Barney understand this and are alert as they go about nibbling on the clover flowers. It is important for cottontail rabbits to learn these lessons well. If they stay still, their color is hard to spot among the plants on the ground. When they run, their white tails are easy to see. That's why being fast and learning to zigzag are important.

Rodney slowly trails behind his family in search of food. He is busy thinking whatever rabbits think on nice spring days. He isn't thinking about danger. Mother Rabbit, sampling tender plants in a garden, is a distance ahead. She thinks all three of her bunnies are nearby. As she raises her head and looks about, she sees Midge and Barney. Where is Rodney?

6

Just then, Mother Rabbit sees that brown and white animal bounding across the yard. A man is throwing a stick, which the animal chases. When the animal reaches the stick, it rushes back to the man with it. Suddenly, the stick lands close to Rodney. He neither stays still nor runs away. He is curious about what looks like a fun game to him. Maybe he can play, too.

Mother Rabbit thumps her foot, but Rodney doesn't pay any attention. She fears that these two big animals might harm her son. She sees that Midge and Barney have darted off toward their den.

Bertha Rabbit goes into action. She makes a few high leaps into the air to attract the attention of the two animals. Both turn in her direction. The man stands still, but the dog decides to give chase. Bertha's strong legs make it easy for her to stay ahead of the barking dog. She leads it away from her den and young ones. Then, she dives under a wooden fence. The dog sniffs and barks, but can't squeeze under the fence.

In the confusion, Rodney takes off and reaches the den. Soon, Mother Rabbit returns to the den when all is quiet. Rodney is shaking. He knows that his mother's actions saved him from harm. She could have been hurt because of him.

If Rodney could speak, he would have told his mother how sorry he was for causing trouble. Since he can't speak, he will just have to show her that he has learned his lesson. Rodney may still daydream and lie in the shade. But he will be more alert and listen for Mother Rabbit's thumping warning sign. ∎

1. Which happens first in the story?

   A Rodney looks at the stick.

   B Mother thumps her foot.

   C Rodney sits under a bush.

   D Mother runs under a fence.

HELPFUL HINT
This question asks you to recall something from a specific area in the passage. Can you remember what happened in the beginning of the story? If you're not sure of the answer, reread the first few paragraphs.

2. How does Rodney act in the story?

   A funny

   B brave

   C worried

   D careless

HELPFUL HINT
This question asks you to think about how a character was acting in the passage. Look at your answer options. Which one best described Rodney based on his actions in the story?

3. The large brown and white animal is *most likely* a

   A cat.

   B dog.

   C mouse.

   D horse.

HELPFUL HINT
This question asks you to draw a conclusion based on information you have learned from reading the passage. What clues does the author give you about what the brown and white animal is?

4. How does Mother Rabbit warn her children of danger?

   A by moving her tail

   B by thumping her foot

   C by closing her eyes

   D by touching her nose

HELPFUL HINT

This question asks you to remember a detail from the passage. Can you recall what Mother Rabbit would do to warn her children? If you are unsure of the answer, reread the fifth paragraph.

5. What does the word "sampling" mean in paragraph six?

   A trying

   B moving

   C planting

   D seeing

HELPFUL HINT

This question asks you to select the meaning of the word "sampling." Reread the sentence in paragraph 6 that uses the underlined word. Are there any clues to the word's meaning in the other sentences in that paragraph?

6. What lesson does Rodney learn at the end of the story?

   A to daydream less

   B to be more careful

   C to eat much faster

   D to move quickly

HELPFUL HINT

This question asks you to guess based on what you have read in the passage. After what he has been through in the passage, how do you think Rodney will act in the future?

FOR THE OPEN-ENDED QUESTION BELOW, REMEMBER TO:
• Pay attention to what the question is asking you.
• Be sure to answer everything the question asks you.
• Fully explain what you mean by your answer.
• Use details from the story.

7. **How is this rabbit family like a human family? Be sure to use examples from the story or your own life to support your answer.**

_____

_____

_____

_____

_____

_____

_____

_____

_____

_____

_____

_____

_____

_____

_____

_____

_____

_____

YOU TRY IT

A Garden Visitor

Usually when people hear the word, "rodent," they think of a rat or a mouse. There are, however, quite a few other animals known as rodents. One of these is the chipmunk or ground squirrel.

One sunny winter day a small striped face poked through the foot-deep snow. Its eyes took in the sights: no danger.

Out popped a small chipmunk. After a short trip, its pouches were filled with birdseed that had been scattered on the ground. Then, it hurried back through the hole in the snow. Probably the warm sun brought the chipmunk out of its burrow. Through the winter months, it lived in burrows safe from the snow and biting cold. It ate the food it had stored before the winter.

During spring and summer, the chipmunk hurries about in search of food. It easily finds nuts, insects, and grains to eat. Sometimes it finds the eggs of ground-nesting birds. Somehow, as fall changes into winter, it knows food will be gone. That's when its large jaw pouches are most useful. It gathers up large amounts of food in those pouches and carries it back to its underground home.

With the coming of March, the female chipmunk is ready to have its young. It takes 31 days for the litter to be born. There are three to five babies in each litter. By about July, the babies are able to care for themselves. By the following spring, those females will have their own litters.

CHECKING FOR UNDERSTANDING
Why do you think chipmunks store up food for winter?

Chipmunks are diggers. They dig in flower boxes for food. They dig in gardens, loosening up small plants. Most of all they dig holes everywhere in the yard. These tunnels lead to their burrows.

7 Among animals visiting our gardens, chipmunks are rather timid creatures. However, if a person sits quite still, a chipmunk may come very close to you. It may even stop, tilt its head, and stare up at you. Perhaps chipmunks feel that with their speed they can quickly outrun danger.

These reddish-brown creatures with their white-and black-striped backs and tails are fun to watch. Since they are small and close to the ground, they need a way to see their surroundings. By standing up tall on their hind legs, they can check the surrounding land. They also have the ability to remain motionless, not even blinking their eyes, for long periods of time. They look almost like garden statues. ■

1. **What *most likely* brought the chipmunk out of its burrow?**

   A cold snow

   B birdseed

   C the warm sun

   D the garden

HELPFUL HINT
This question asks you to recall an assumption the author made in paragraph 3. Can you remember the reason why the chipmunk would leave his burrow?

2. **Why is it important for a chipmunk to collect nuts and seeds in the fall?**

   A They are used to make warm nests for the winter.

   B They are used to keep other animals away.

   C The chipmunk does not like eating any other foods.

   D The chipmunk will not be able to find any in the winter.

HELPFUL HINT
This question asks you to guess based on what you have read. Can you imagine why it would be important for the chipmunk to gather food in the fall? What reason would the chipmunk have for doing this?

3. **The chipmunk uses its pouches to**

   A escape enemies.

   B build nests.

   C gather food.

   D dig holes.

HELPFUL HINT
This question asks you to remember a detail from the passage. Where did the passage mention the chipmunk's pouches? If you are unsure about the answer, reread the fourth paragraph.

4. **What does the word "timid" mean in paragraph 7?**

   A silly

   B sad

   C shy

   D slow

HELPFUL HINT

This question asks you to select the meaning of the word "timid." Reread the sentence in paragraph 7 that uses the underlined word. Are there any clues to the word's meaning in the other sentences in that paragraph?

5. **What must you do to get close to a chipmunk?**

   A keep very still

   B run very fast

   C talk very softly

   D stay very low

HELPFUL HINT

This question asks you to remember a detail from the passage. Look back at the passage for a description of how chipmunks react to people.

6. **The purpose of the eighth paragraph is to**

   A tell where chipmunks live.

   B explain what chipmunks look like.

   C explain what chipmunks eat.

   D tell why chipmunks enjoy digging

HELPFUL HINT

This question asks you to guess based on what you have read. Can you imagine why the author included paragraph 8? What did paragraph 8 tell you?

FOR THE OPEN-ENDED QUESTION BELOW, REMEMBER TO:
• Pay attention to what the question is asking you.
• Be sure to answer everything the question asks you.
• Fully explain what you mean by your answer.
• Use details from the passage.

7. **Name at least four kinds of food that chipmunks eat. Explain how a chipmunk carries its food and what it is described as preparing for in the passage. Use specific examples from the passage to make your answer very descriptive.**

_____

_____

_____

_____

_____

_____

_____

_____

_____

_____

_____

_____

_____

YOU TRY IT

> **DIRECTIONS:** Read this passage, and answer the questions that follow.

John James Audubon

John James Audubon was known as a famous painter of birds. Many books of his paintings were printed. A bird picture often took up a full page. This gave a detailed view of the bird. Printing these volumes took years.

Audubon is known for his paintings of United States' birds. However, few people know much about him. In 1785, John James Audubon was born on the island of Haiti to a Creole mother and a French father. At the age of five, he went to France for his education. It was there that he began drawing birds. At the age of eighteen, he had to go into the French Army. Instead, his father sent him to the United States to work.

For the next fifteen years, John had many jobs. He tried his hand at mining and at running a general store. His art skills were used to paint portraits and to teach drawing. He even worked at stuffing animals. This is called "taxidermy." All the while, as he studied and painted birds, he managed to travel from Florida to Canada.

In 1824, John went to Europe to get his bird pictures published. At that time, Europe was where the best publishers were. He found a publisher in Scotland. From that time until 1839, he traveled between Europe and the U.S.

 CHECKING FOR UNDERSTANDING

Why do you think the author included information about John Audubon's previous jobs?

Then, he settled in New York. For the rest of his life, John worked on his books. They showed hundreds of his paintings of birds and of other animals. Although John died in 1851, these books are still highly prized today. ∎

1. **Where did John James Audubon go to school?**

   A   Haiti

   B   Scotland

   C   France

   D   United States

   HELPFUL HINT
   This question asks you to recall a detail from the passage. Can you remember where in the passage you were told about John going to school? If you are unsure of the answer, reread the second paragraph.

2. **How did traveling help John James Audubon?**

   A   He got books printed.

   B   He met his mother.

   C   He joined the army.

   D   He saw more birds.

   HELPFUL HINT
   This question asks you to draw a conclusion based on information you have learned from reading the passage. Is there anything that John did on his travels that would have helped him?

3. **Which job helped John James Audubon to make his pictures of birds better?**

   A   teaching drawing

   B   running a store

   C   mining

   D   traveling

   HELPFUL HINT
   This question asks you to make a guess about which of John's many jobs helped his pictures of birds to become better. Look at your choices. Which one do you think would have helped you if you were John?

4. Why did John James Audubon's father send him to the United States?

   A to go to school

   B to start working

   C to publish a book

   D to see his mother

HELPFUL HINT
This question asks you to recall a detail from the passage. If you are unsure of the answer, reread the second and third paragraphs. You should look for a mention of John first arriving in the United States.

5. Why are John James Audubon's books valuable today?

   A They were made in the 1800s.

   B They were printed in Europe.

   C They show detailed views of birds.

   D They show pictures of the whole country.

HELPFUL HINT
This question asks you to draw a conclusion based on information you have learned from reading the passage. What do you think makes John's books so valuable?

6. In which genre is the passage "John James Audubon"?

   A narrative about early U.S. exploration

   B narrative about a man's life and work

   C everyday text to introduce bird watching

   D everyday text about the art of taxidermy

HELPFUL HINT
This question asks you to think about what kind of passage you have just read. How would you describe this passage to someone who hasn't read it?

FOR THE OPEN-ENDED QUESTION BELOW, REMEMBER TO:
- Pay attention to what the question is asking you.
- Be sure to answer everything the question asks you.
- Fully explain what you mean by your answer.
- Use details from the passage.

7. What do you think of John James Audubon's paintings and books? Did he do something valuable for others? Support your statements with details from the passage.

_____

_____

_____

_____

_____

_____

_____

_____

_____

_____

_____

_____

Chapter 4: **Expanding the Text**
Author's Point of View

We have already learned about identifying the author's purpose for writing what you read. We have also learned that sometimes there is a deeper meaning to the text. In this chapter, you will learn about the meaning of text.

In this chapter you will also work on two very important skills: **questioning** and **predicting**. These are both very important skills because they help you develop a strong understanding of what you are reading before, while, and after you read.

RL.3.6: NARRATOR OR SPEAKER'S POINT OF VIEW
RI.3.8: AUTHOR'S REASONS AND EVIDENCE

You Try It

Your teacher hands you a book. The title is "The Golden Crown." She asks you to predict what this story is about. How do you develop your prediction?

• Do you flip through the pages and look at the illustrations?

• Do you read the title and think about what it might mean?

• Do you read the first few pages of the book?

One good way to check your understanding of a story is to stop from time-to-time to ask yourself, "Is my prediction right?" If it is not right, what is different?

How can I predict meaning?

It may happen that you will read something on the ASK4 that you don't quite understand. Sometimes it is unclear what an author means by his or her words. You might have to figure out for yourself what the author really means. You might be asked to guess, or predict, what the meaning of a word or sentence is.

In some cases, it might seem that something you read could actually mean more than one thing. For example, read these sentences:

At this point, Miranda was really frustrated. She couldn't believe how lost she was! She wondered if she'd ever figure it out.

The meaning of these sentences is unclear. This is because we do not know the context of the sentences. In other words, we don't know what's going on around them. Depending on what has happened to Miranda before this point or what happens after, the meaning of the words could be very different.

For instance, imagine Miranda is actually in math class trying to figure out a division problem. In that case, she must feel lost as to how to solve the problem. That is why she is frustrated.

But what if Miranda is actually in the woods? In that case she must be physically lost. In other words she does not know where she is or in which direction to go. She is frustrated because she can't seem to find her way out of the woods.

As you can see, the context of words can change their meaning.

LET'S TRY IT TOGETHER

DIRECTIONS: Read this sentence from a story about a boy facing a challenge and we'll discuss the questions together.

"I'm afraid my legs would freeze together and I wouldn't be able to walk."

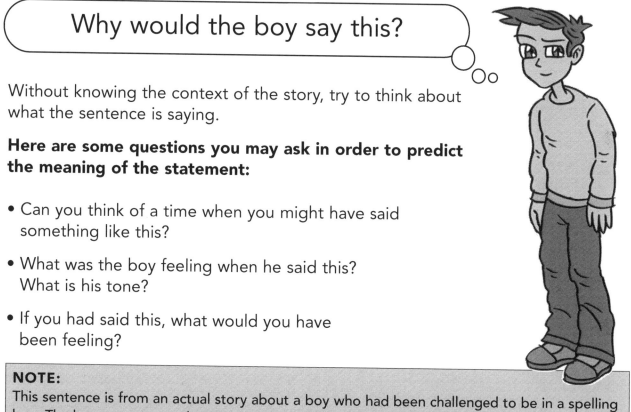

Why would the boy say this?

Without knowing the context of the story, try to think about what the sentence is saying.

Here are some questions you may ask in order to predict the meaning of the statement:

• Can you think of a time when you might have said something like this?

• What was the boy feeling when he said this? What is his tone?

• If you had said this, what would you have been feeling?

NOTE:
This sentence is from an actual story about a boy who had been challenged to be in a spelling bee. The boy got more and more nervous as the date of the spelling bee approached.

What is questioning?

We have already discussed how important it is to think about what you are reading. A good way to do this is to think of questions about the text. This is called questioning.

Questioning means to seek information.

The goal of any question you ask would be to learn more about the passage or the author's purpose.

Sometimes you may want to ask a question of a character in the story. At other times, you may wish to ask the author a question.

How do I ask good questions?

Asking a good question is not easy. You have to carefully think before you ask a question.

Here are some tips for asking good questions:

Think about what you want to know.

Sometimes you may not be able to ask more than one question. You should choose each question carefully to make sure that you will find out what you want to know.

Be sure to word your question carefully.

If the question is unclear, you may not get the answer for which you're looking.

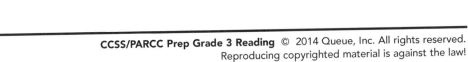

Why is it important to understand everything I read?

Sometimes what you read is complicated and hard to understand. You may want to stop after reading parts of the story and ask yourself if you've understood what the story is saying.

This is important when you are trying to explain what you have read and when you are asked questions about the text.

Here are questions that you may be asked that would require you to make something more clear:

• What is the theme or central idea of the passage?

• Is this true?

• How does the author think or feel about the topic?

• How did the writer approach the topic?

• Who do you think is the audience the author was trying to reach?

• Compare and contrast by telling what is the same and what is different in the text.

How can I predict what will happen?

Predicting means expecting something to happen, telling what is going to happen, and being prepared for the outcome.

Your personal experiences will help you predict events in a story. You may be able to guess what will happen next in a story if you have been in a similar situation yourself. You can also use context clues, or clues found in the text, to make predictions about the story. This skill is almost always used in open-ended questions.

How can you tell what will happen next in a story?

Sometimes you will be reading only part of a story and you will have to answer a question about what will happen next.

It is important to ask questions about a text before, while, and after you read. You might ask:

Before Reading: *What is this story going to be about?*

While Reading: *Why does Jack decide to stay home from school?*

After Reading: *Did I understand everything about the story?*

Questioning helps you know what has happened so far in a story. It helps you make predictions about what might happen next. It helps you make a personal connection with the text.

STORY SUMMARY:
In a story about a family whose home was flooded, you read about the hurricane that brought the strong winds and the heavy rain. You learn what the family was able to take with them when they had to leave their house. The story ends as the family is on their way back to see what is left of their home. You are asked to write about the family's experience, beginning when they first heard the hurricane warning, and then to tell what they will do next.

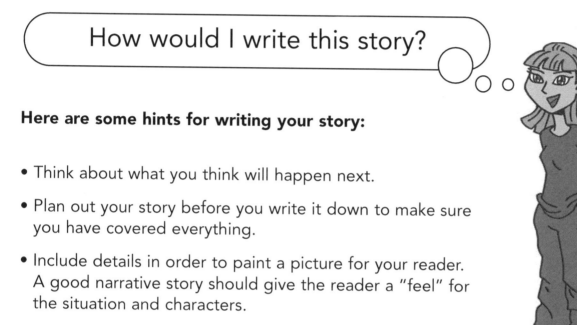

How would I write this story?

Here are some hints for writing your story:

• Think about what you think will happen next.

• Plan out your story before you write it down to make sure you have covered everything.

• Include details in order to paint a picture for your reader. A good narrative story should give the reader a "feel" for the situation and characters.

LET'S TRY IT TOGETHER

DIRECTIONS: Read the paragraphs below and we'll discuss the questions together.

Two girls strolled down the beach road, talking as they walked along. They passed some cottages and then, as they came around a bend in the road, they saw a large barn. The barn was very old and it certainly didn't look like it was being used.

As the girls were standing there, they heard tiny "mew, mew" sounds coming from inside the barn. They wanted to go inside to look but neither one was sure that it would be the right thing to do. ■

What will happen next in the story?

Here are some questions you may ask in order to predict the outcome of the story:

- What will happen next?

- Will the girls decide to go into the barn or not? If they don't, what will they do instead? If they do, what will they see inside?

- How would you write the next part of this story?

NOTE:
Based on the clues in the story, you could guess that the girls will go in the barn and find a cat or a kitten. Or they could go home and tell an adult and come back to investigate further.

YOU TRY IT

DIRECTIONS: Read the story below and we'll discuss the questions together.

A Costume Party

Myra's favorite holiday is Halloween. She is very creative and loves to make her own costumes. This year her parents said she could have a Halloween party rather than going trick-or-treating. Myra was so excited!

She made her own invitations to the party, letting her friends know that it would be a costume party. It wasn't your usual costume party, though. She wanted everyone who attended to make their own costumes. At the end of the party there would be a vote and everyone would decide who was wearing the best costume. ■

1. **What do you think is going to happen at the party?**

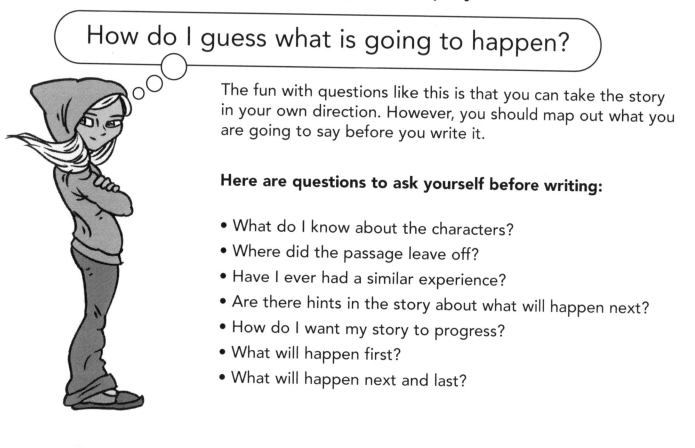

How do I guess what is going to happen?

The fun with questions like this is that you can take the story in your own direction. However, you should map out what you are going to say before you write it.

Here are questions to ask yourself before writing:

- What do I know about the characters?
- Where did the passage leave off?
- Have I ever had a similar experience?
- Are there hints in the story about what will happen next?
- How do I want my story to progress?
- What will happen first?
- What will happen next and last?

2. **Think of all the costumes that you imagine would be at the party. Describe those costumes in as much detail as you can.**

How can I describe costumes?

Here, you get to use your imagination. Your goal is to make your reader picture the image you are describing.

Here are questions to ask yourself before writing:

- Have you ever been to a costume party?
- What kind of costumes did you see?
- What do the costumes look like?
- What do the costumes feel like?
- Are they shiny? Are they slippery-looking?
- Are they thick or heavy? Are they light and airy?

Write your answers below and on the next page.

_____

_____

_____

_____

_____

_____

_____

What is imagery?

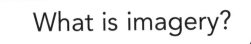

One way that writers improve their writing is by including imagery.

Imagery means the use of language to paint a picture, or image, in a reader's mind.

Example: The rose was as red as a freshly cleaned fire engine.

In this sentence the author is using imagery to help the reader imagine how red the rose looked.

Sometimes writers use imagery to help a reader get a better picture of what is happening in a story.

Example: The dog spun around and around like a spinning top trying to catch his own tail.

In this example the author uses a funny description to help the reader understand what is happening in the story.

Two common types of imagery that writers use are similes and metaphors. Both compare two different things in a creative and imaginative way.

What is a simile?

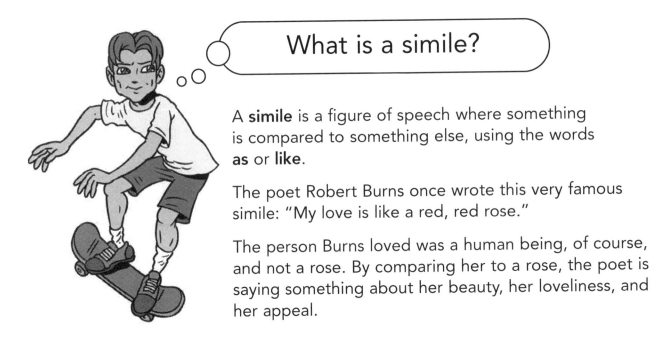

A **simile** is a figure of speech where something is compared to something else, using the words **as** or **like**.

The poet Robert Burns once wrote this very famous simile: "My love is like a red, red rose."

The person Burns loved was a human being, of course, and not a rose. By comparing her to a rose, the poet is saying something about her beauty, her loveliness, and her appeal.

Read these examples of similes.

- My feet are as warm as toast.
- The tiny little girl is as light as a feather.
- Melanie looked as pretty as a picture.
- My brother was as cool as a cucumber.
- The winner of the race ran like the wind.
- The grimy mechanic had been working like a dog.
- Larry's temper was as explosive as a volcano.
- Playing chess with Dad is like trying to outsmart a computer.

You might want to ask yourself these questions about similes:

- Is this the first time you have heard similes like these?
- Have you ever used similes yourself?
- Do you ever compare something to another thing?

Now it's your turn!

Try to write a few similes yourself. Remember that similes have to compare two things. You also have to use either the word **as** or the word **like** in each one.

_____

_____

_____

_____

_____

_____

What is a metaphor?

The second figure of speech we are going to talk about is the **metaphor**.

A metaphor is also a comparison. However, it does not use the words **as** or **like** in the same way a simile does.

Like similes, you have probably already heard and used metaphors in your speech and in your writing.

Read these examples of metaphors.

- It is raining cats and dogs.
- Mary's cousin Juliet is a star.
- My mom told me that my bedroom is a disaster area.
- Kitty is the apple of her mother's eye.

Here are some things to consider about these metaphors:

- Do any of them sound familiar?
- How many are new to you?

Now it's your turn!

Try to write a few metaphors yourself. Keep in mind that sometimes a very complicated thing is compared to a simpler thing in order to make the more complicated thing easier to understand.

_____

_____

_____

What is sarcasm?

Sarcasm is when someone says, or writes, something but really means the opposite of what he or she said or wrote.

Example: "Oh, I just **love** Monday mornings,"
Sheri said as she slowly rolled out of bed.

What Sheri really means is:
I cannot stand Monday mornings.

Example: "I **can't wait** until I can go to the dentist's office again." Jacob said after getting a tooth pulled.

What Jacob really means is:
I never want to go to the dentist again.

Sometimes writers use sarcasm and humor to help make their writing more exciting and entertaining.

Now it's your turn!

Try to write a sarcastic statement. Then write the real meaning of the statement underneath it.

Statement:

_____

Real Meaning:

_____

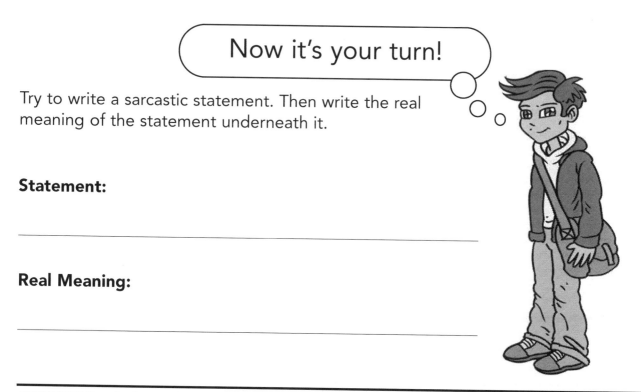

YOU TRY IT

DIRECTIONS: Read this story, and answer the questions that follow.

The Case of the Missing Chocolates

Mrs. Walters opened a cellophane bag. She filled the candy dish with chocolates. Each was wrapped in colorful foil. It was something she did for company or at holiday time. She would have done it more often except for her husband, Mr. Walters. He was on a diet and loved chocolate. So, it seemed cruel to have candy around.

After their guests left on Saturday evening, the candy dish was more than three-quarters full. By Monday evening, Mrs. Walters saw that the dish didn't seem as full. "George, have you been eating candy?" she inquired. ⌉ 2

"No, I haven't," he replied. "Why do you ask?"

"Well, I thought there was more candy in the dish. That's all," she answered. "I guess I'm mistaken."

As she picked up the newspapers the next evening, she glanced at the candy dish. Again, it seemed that there were fewer pieces of candy.

"That George!" she thought to herself. When he entered the room she asked teasingly, "George, are you sure you haven't been eating these chocolates? I know there were more candies here yesterday."

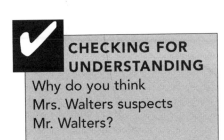

CHECKING FOR UNDERSTANDING

Why do you think Mrs. Walters suspects Mr. Walters?

He heaved a sigh. "I told you I haven't been eating them. I have been tempted, though. Maybe it's one of the children."

Mrs. Walters didn't worry about them eating the candy. Out of curiosity, though, she did ask them. All three of them said they hadn't eaten it.

Every day more and more of the candy was missing. Now the whole family was interested. It was a mystery. How was the candy disappearing? There were no signs of the foil wrappers anywhere.

By the end of the week, the dish was empty. Mrs. Walters decided not to refill the dish. However, the mystery of the disappearing candy remained.

The Walters had been trying to give a sofa away. The following week, Mr. Walters announced that a friend was interested in it. He and his son would come by on Saturday with their pickup truck. Mrs. Walters was delighted to be rid of the heavy sleeper sofa. Before they took it, though, she wanted to make sure it was clean.

"George, come help me move the sofa away from the wall," she called. She had already vacuumed the cushions. Now she wanted to do the back of the sofa.

They pulled the sofa away from the wall. There they found a small pile of colorful foil bits. No chocolates, just empty foil wrappers. "Mice!" they both exclaimed.

They hadn't been bothered by little field mice for a long time. One mouse that liked chocolates had gotten into the house. The mystery of the missing chocolates was solved. Now, all that remained was to solve the problem of getting rid of their unwanted guest. ■

1. **Why doesn't Mrs. Walters usually keep chocolate in the dish?**

   A She doesn't have very many people over to the house.

   B She wants to help Mr. Walters stay on his diet.

   C She doesn't think that chocolates taste good.

   D She thinks that the children will eat them all.

HELPFUL HINT
This question asks you to draw a conclusion based on information you have learned from reading the passage. What reason does Mrs. Walters have for not keeping chocolate in the dish?

2. **What does the word "inquired" mean in paragraph two?**

   A bothered

   B yelled

   C taught

   D asked

HELPFUL HINT
This question asks you to select the meaning of the word "inquired". Reread the sentence in the second paragraph that uses the underlined word. Are there any clues in the other sentences in that paragraph or in others to the word's meaning?

3. **How does Mrs. Walters *most likely* feel when she sees more candy missing?**

   A frightened

   B happy

   C surprised

   D lonely

HELPFUL HINT
This question asks you to guess based on what you have read in the passage. Mrs. Walters didn't expect to see the candy missing. What do you think her reaction was when she noticed that it was missing?

4. **What does Mrs. Walters want to do before giving the sofa away?**

   A She wants to clean the sofa.

   B She wants to put the sofa outside.

   C She wants to take the sofa apart.

   D She wants to sew the sofa.

⭐ **HELPFUL HINT**
This question asks you to recall a detail from the passage. If you are unsure of the answer, reread the last few paragraphs. You should look for a mention of giving the sofa away.

5. **How does Mrs. Walters discover where the chocolates went?**

   A by asking the children

   B by asking Mr. Walters

   C by moving the sofa

   D by cleaning the house

⭐ **HELPFUL HINT**
This question asks you to recall a detail From the passage. Do you remember how Mrs. Walters figures out where the chocolates went? If you are unsure of the answer, reread the end of the passage.

6. **What is the next problem the Walters must face?**

   A getting more chocolates

   B getting rid of the mouse

   C moving the sofa outside

   D moving out of their house

⭐ **HELPFUL HINT**
This question asks you to predict what will happen next in the story.
If you were one of the Walters, what would your next step be?

FOR THE OPEN-ENDED QUESTION BELOW, REMEMBER TO:
- Pay attention to what the question is asking you.
- Be sure to answer everything the question asks you.
- Fully explain what you mean by your answer.
- Use details from the story.

7. Based on what you've read in the story, what do you think the Walters family will do to catch the creature that has been eating the chocolates from their candy dish? How do you think it will turn out in the end? Will they succeed? Use information from the story to support your response.

YOU TRY IT

> **DIRECTIONS:** Read this passage and answer the questions that follow.
> **INTRODUCTION:** This letter was in the local newspaper after the magic show benefit for Dashawn Washington.

Letter to the Editor

| Sunday, April 10 | THE LAKEFIELD TIMES | F5 |

EDITORIAL

"Benefit Program is Worthwhile"

Dear Editor:

I am writing concerning an action taken by the Board of Education. On Monday night, they voted not to allow a benefit program performance at the high school.

The benefit, sponsored by the Dashawn Fund, was to be a fund-raiser for the Washington family. Their son was seriously injured in a bike accident this year. Dashawn will need four operations on his leg. Even then, he may not be able to walk again. The money from the benefit program would have been used to help his family pay for the costly operations.

Yet, the board turned it down, even though it had been started by Field School, a school within its own district.

I firmly believe that this is a worthwhile program.

"The benefit . . . was to be a fund-raiser for the Washington family [whose] son was seriously injured in a bike accident this year."

The students requesting the benefit are Dashawn's classmates. They had a detailed plan and even offered to make changes to the plan. In spite of this, the board refused in less time than it takes to read this letter.

I do not understand this decision. The Williams Troupe are students, not professionals.

We are sure that the show would be a big success. The audience really loved it when it was performed at Field Elementary School just last month.

The evening was filled with fun. The student magicians did an excellent job. Mr. Williams had done a great job teaching the students magic tricks.

After the program was performed at Field School, parents suggested another show be given at the high school. They felt that this would raise more money for the Dashawn Fund.

Everyone thought that it was a great idea. Parents volunteered to present the idea at a board meeting. They were surprised at the board's decision. This is a win-win project. The money raised would go for a good cause. As I said, Dashawn's family needs the money. They cannot pay for all of the operations.

(see **Benefit**, continued on page **F6**)

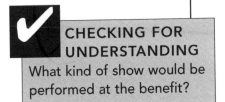

CHECKING FOR UNDERSTANDING
What kind of show would be performed at the benefit?

Sunday, April 10 | THE LAKEFIELD TIMES | F6

Editorial

Benefit (from page **F5**)

The students in Mrs. Jones's class would benefit from putting on this program. They would be helping one of their classmates in need.

Besides learning how to plan a large event, students would gain experience performing tricks. One of them might even become a professional magician!

The board gave two reasons for their decision. The first was that the high school auditorium could not be used on the date requested because of summer renovations.

Parking was their other concern. The auditorium parking lots will be closed while work is being done at the high school.

I believe that these were weak reasons to reject the program. It was as if the board had already made their decision before the students spoke.

There is an answer to both concerns: change the date of the program. Construction at the high school begins in late June. If the program was held in May, the high school could be used. I am sure the students would agree.

I ask you to invite Mrs. Jones's class to your next board meeting. Together, you and the students can find a way to address your concerns. This would be democracy in action.

In other words, students would be given a chance to see that two groups that disagree can and should come together peaceably and discuss their differences. In this way, we can come to an agreement that might make us both happy. For the students, it would also be a positive lesson in how government can work.

Yours truly,

Joanne Williams

1. **Why did Mrs. Jones's class start the Dashawn Fund?**

   A to let a class learn magic

   B to raise money for a school

   C to help a hurt student

   D to teach bike safety to kids

   HELPFUL HINT
   This question asks you to recall a detail from the passage. Can you remember why the Dashawn Fund was started? If you are unsure of the answer, reread the early paragraphs.

2. **How did *most* people feel when the board would not let the students put on the show?**

   A worried

   B surprised

   C excited

   D pleased

   HELPFUL HINT
   This questions asks you to make a guess based on what you read in the passage. Look at your answer options. How would you feel if you had been one of the students in the Williams Troupe?

3. **Who taught the students magic tricks?**

   A Mr. Washington

   B Mrs. Jones

   C Mr. Williams

   D Mrs. Williams

   HELPFUL HINT
   This question asks you to recall a detail from the article. If you are unsure of the answer, reread the seventh paragraph. You should look for a mention of who had taught the students.

4. **What did the parents do after the show at the elementary school?**

   A They asked the students how the magic tricks were done.

   B They told the students that they should hold many more shows.

   C They asked the students where they had learned the magic tricks.

   D They told the students they should perform at the high school.

HELPFUL HINT

This question asks you to remember something mentioned in the passage. If you are unsure of the answer, skim the passage. You should look for where the author mentions the parents talking to the students.

5. **What does the word "gain" mean in paragraph eleven?**

   A see

   B need

   C get

   D take

HELPFUL HINT

This question asks you to select the meaning of the word "gain." Reread the sentence in the paragraph that uses the underlined word. Are there any clues to the word's meaning in the other sentences in that paragraph?

6. **Why can't the students have the magic show at the high school?**

   A The high school is being updated.

   B The high school is not big enough.

   C The high school is closed during the summer.

   D The high school is not close enough to town.

HELPFUL HINT

This question asks you to recall a detail from the passage. What was the reason why the students could not perform in the high school? If you are unsure of the answer, reread the paragraph about why the board made its decision.

FOR THE OPEN-ENDED QUESTION BELOW, REMEMBER TO:
- Pay attention to what the question is asking you.
- Be sure to answer everything the question asks you.
- Fully explain what you mean by your answer.
- Use details from the passage.

7. **What is the author trying to say in the last paragraph of this Letter to the Editor? Explain.**

_____

_____

_____

_____

_____

_____

_____

_____

_____

_____

_____

_____

_____

_____

YOU TRY IT

DIRECTIONS: Read this story, and answer the questions that follow.

Great Minds Think Alike

Julie and Michele are best friends. They like all of the same things and do everything together. Together, they started their own afterschool bake sale to earn money. With the money they raised, they planned on buying two brand new identical scooters.

After two weeks of baking and selling, they finally had earned enough money for the scooters. The two girls were so excited that they closed the bake sale early and headed straight for the scooter shop.

3 "We will take those two," Julie said with a gleaming smile. She was pointing to the two most beautiful scooters in the shop. They were sitting on a platform in the window and had a spotlight shining on them. They were as bright red as a beautiful rose in full bloom. The silvery metal on them glimmered in the spotlight.

After they left the shop, the two girls tried out their scooters. They rode to the park, then to library, then to the playground. They had so much fun. There was only one problem. Every time they got off of their scooters they couldn't figure out which scooter belonged to Julie and which belonged to Michele.

"Oh no," Michele said. "We didn't think about the fact that our scooters are exactly the same. What are we going to do?"

The two girls didn't know what they should do.

That night, Julie was at home thinking about the day's events. All of sudden she had a great idea.

"I've got it!" Julie said to herself. "I know how to make my scooter different than Michele's." She was so excited she ran downstairs and started on her big idea.

Meanwhile at Michele's house, she too was thinking about her great day. Then she remembered her problem. "How can I make my scooter different than Julie's," Michele thought to herself. "Wait…I've got it." Michele ran outside to her scooter.

The next day Michele ran the doorbell at Julie's house. Julie bound down the steps to open the door for her. "Why hello there Michele," Julie said with a smile that went from ear to ear.

"Hi, Julie," Michele said back with an equally large grin.

"I figured out how to make my bike different," both girls said at the exact same time.

"Wait, what did you say?" Michele asked.

"I solved our problem," Julie told her. "My scooter doesn't look like yours anymore."

"No, I solved our problem," Michele stated.

The two girls looked at each other confused.

"Go get your scooter," Michele told Julie.

Julie pulled her scooter out from the garage. She placed it right next to Michele's scooter. The two girls looked at each other in shock. They couldn't believe it. They both started laughing uncontrollably.

There they were, Michele's bright blue scooter, and Julie's bright blue scooter. The two looked like two big blueberries sitting next to each other.

"Oh, now we will definitely be able to tell our scooters apart," Julie said laughing.

"I guess great minds really do think alike," Michele laughed.

The two girls smiled at each other, got on their scooters and rode to school. ∎

1. **At the beginning of the story what is Julie and Michele's goal?**

   A   to paint their scooters different colors

   B   to buy different scooters for each other

   C   to ride their scooters all the way to school

   D   to sell enough baked goods to buy a scooter

   ⭐ **HELPFUL HINT**
   This question asks you recall information from the selection. Can you find where this information is in the story? There is a hint word in the question itself.

2. **What do the two girls learn about each other?**

   A   They often think alike.

   B   They are good at baking.

   C   They both hate the color red.

   D   They like to trick each other.

   ⭐ **HELPFUL HINT**
   This question asks about the characters' relationship. What do you know about the two girls? If you are unsure of the answer, reread the last few sentences of the story.

3. **Why does Julie say: "Oh, now we will definitely be able to tell our scooters apart?"**

   A   She is angry that Michele copied her idea.

   B   She thinks the two scooters look different.

   C   She is making a joke about their scooters.

   D   She does not know which scooter is hers.

   ⭐ **HELPFUL HINT**
   This question asks you to think about the meaning of a character's statement. How do you think Julie feels about what has happened?

4. **What funny thing do the girls do in this story?**

    A buy two different types of scooters

    B paint their scooters the same color

    C ride their scooters to the playground

    D start their own afterschool bake sale

⭐ **HELPFUL HINT**
This question asks about something funny that happens in this story. Do each of the answer options happen in the story? The ones that do happen, are they all funny?

5. **Reread paragraph three in the story. What is the author comparing?**

    A a flower and a rose

    B a rose and the scooters

    C the color red and a rose

    D the color red and the scooters

⭐ **HELPFUL HINT**
This question asks you to identify what the author is comparing in these sentences. Can you tell why the author mentions a rose in these sentences? What image is the author trying to paint in the reader's mind?

6. **Which sentence does the author include to show that the girls think that what they did was funny?**

    A "The two girls didn't know what they should do."

    B "Julie said with a smile that went from ear to ear."

    C "The two girls looked at each other confused."

    D "They both started laughing uncontrollably."

⭐ **HELPFUL HINT**
This question asks you to identify how an author shows something is funny. Think about what people do when they think something is funny.

FOR THE OPEN-ENDED QUESTION BELOW, REMEMBER TO:
• Pay attention to what the question is asking you.
• Be sure to answer everything the question asks you.
• Fully explain what you mean by your answer.
• Use details from the story.

7. The author describes the scooters in many ways in this story to help the reader get a better picture of it. Give at least two ways the author describes the scooter. Then explain how each helps the reader picture the scooter.

_____

_____

_____

_____

_____

_____

_____

_____

_____

_____

_____

_____

_____

YOU TRY IT

DIRECTIONS: Read this passage, and answer the questions that follow.

Putting on Your Own Magic Show

Plan Your Show

Since you are planning a magic show, you already know how to do a number of magic tricks. However, to have a successful show, you must have a plan for the show. This plan includes choosing the tricks you will do and deciding what you will say and l wear. The following list will help as you start your planning.

1. **Make a list of the tricks you will use.** You have been practicing magic tricks for a while. Now you need to select the ones you will use in your magic show. Choose ones that you feel comfortable performing and those your friends will enjoy seeing.

2. **Collect the props and other items needed for the tricks you choose.** Put the props for each trick into a separate box. It is important to have everything needed to do a trick close at hand when you are on the stage. Putting the materials for each trick in a separate box helps to ensure that you have what you will need.

3. **Arrange the magic tricks you have chosen into a logical order.** The order in which you do your tricks is important. Beginning magicians often present the tricks they have learned as they come to mind. Instead, you need to think about the flow of the tricks. Vary the order in which the tricks are done. Ask yourself the question, "How does each one follow a path into the next trick?" This will give a nice routine to your act. Performing different types of tricks also helps maintain audience interest.

Presentation of Magic Tricks

When you perform your magic tricks in front of an audience, you need to be aware of two things. The first is what you will say and how you will act while doing your tricks. The second is what you will wear.

How you act in front of your audience has a big impact on how successful you are. A magician is an actor who entertains people. Think about what to say during each trick. Magicians talk a lot. This helps them to do each trick without people noticing how it was done. The more a magician talks, the better the show.

Make notes on what you want to say about each trick. Think about what to say that would get the audience to look at something you are doing that is not important to doing the trick. Then, practice saying it while doing the trick. Do this in front of a mirror. You will be able to see how you look doing the trick.

How you act on the stage is also important. Always face your audience. The props for your trick must also be within easy reach. These should be either in front of you or to one side. Never turn around to get a prop.

When you do your trick, make sure that you have all the items needed for the trick. Remember to talk while doing the trick. When you are finished with each trick, take a bow. If the trick does not work, make a joke about it. You might even pretend that the mistake was part of the trick.

Finally, think about what you will wear during the magic show. Most magicians wear colorful clothes. A bright jacket and pants make a good magic show outfit.

Summary

Now you are ready to put on your magic show. Remember to keep your show short. It is better to finish with an audience hungry for more tricks. That way, they will come back for your next show. ■

1. **What must you know how to do before you plan a magic show?**

   A how to make colorful clothing

   B how to do some magic tricks

   C how to listen to friends

   D how to work with others

HELPFUL HINT

This question asks you to draw a conclusion. If you were going to put on a magic show, what would you have to know before you plan the show? Recall what the author said in the first paragraph to help you.

2. **What is the first thing you should do when planning a magic show?**

   A collect the props you need

   B think of what you will say

   C put on a colorful jacket

   D make a list of your tricks

HELPFUL HINT

This question asks you to recall a detail from the passage. Do you remember the first step in the planning process? If you are unsure, find the steps and reread them.

3. **How should you feel about the trick you will perform?**

   A You should be comfortable with the trick.

   B You should be frightened by the trick.

   C You should be puzzled by the trick.

   D You should be worried about the trick.

HELPFUL HINT

This question asks you to make a statement based on what you have read in the passage. Look at the answers. Which of them do you think is the way you should feel if you're going to perform a trick?

4. Why do magicians talk a lot?

  A so the magician can tell people what happens next

  B so people can't tell that the magician is scared

  C so the magician can tell people many funny jokes

  D so people can't tell how the magician does the trick

HELPFUL HINT
This question asks you to guess based on what you have read in the passage. What did the story tell you about magicians talking during their tricks? If you are unsure of the answer, reread the passage.

5. Where should you practice your magic show?

  A in front of a friend

  B in front of a mirror

  C in a playhouse

  D in a classroom

HELPFUL HINT
This question asks you to recall a detail from the passage. Can you remember where the passage said to practice? If you are unsure of the answer, skim the passage for clues.

6. What is the *most likely* reason that magicians wear colorful clothes?

  A so people will notice them

  B so they look happy

  C so people can see the tricks

  D so they look scary

HELPFUL HINT
This question asks you to draw a conclusion. What outcome would a magician be looking for by wearing colorful clothes?

FOR THE OPEN-ENDED QUESTION BELOW, REMEMBER TO:
- Pay attention to what the question is asking you.
- Be sure to answer everything the question asks you.
- Fully explain what you mean by your answer.
- Use details from the story.

7. Pretend that you are a magician and that you have just planned a show that you think will be your best yet.
   - Write out the three or four sentences you will say as you introduce yourself and begin your show.
   - Describe one trick that will be part of the show and tell in detail how you will do it.
   - Predict whether or not the audience will like your show.

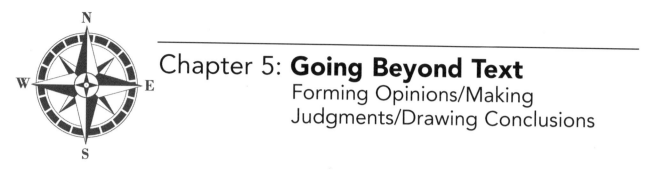

In many questions, you may be asked to **form an opinion** about what you have read. This chapter will teach you how to form an opinion by gathering facts from the text.

Similarly, you may be asked to **make a judgment** or **draw a conclusion**. While those two tasks may sound like they would be the same, there are differences in the way you would approach each. It is important to think out your point of view and plan what you want to say before you answer the questions being asked. You will learn some effective strategies on how to do these things.

RI.3.10: FORMING OF OPINIONS

You Try It

You have just finished reading a story. Your teacher asks you to write your opinion of the actions of one of the characters in the story. What do you do?

- Do you write down what the character looked like?

- Do you write down what the character did?

- Do you write down your feelings about the character?

Your best bet would be to do the last option. You should write about what you thought about what the character did.

What is an opinion?

How often does someone ask you, "What do you think?"

This person is asking for your **opinion**. An opinion is what a person thinks. Opinions are not right or wrong—each person can have his or her own opinion.

A **fact** is based on real information and not just on what someone thinks. You have to be able to tell the difference between a fact and an opinion.

Here are some facts. They are based on real information and can be proven.
- Earth rotates around the sun.
- Chickens lay eggs.
- It is raining today.
- Tom's birthday is next Thursday.

Here are some everyday opinions from students.
- Today's weather is delightful.
- This food is delicious.
- Last night's homework was too difficult.
- My teacher is too strict.
- The new baby is so cute.

Here are questions to ask yourself about these different statements:
- Can you tell the difference between these kinds of statements?
- What lets you know that the facts can be proven?

Ask yourself—could I find out if this is true?
- If the answer is yes, then the statement is a fact.
- If the answer is no, then the statement is an opinion.

When would I be asked for my opinion?

You may be asked to form an opinion about a story or an article you've read. Then you may be asked to back up your answer with facts and information from the text.

Here are examples of this kind of question:

Example: You read about a parade a town holds to honor all the men and women who have worked to protect our country. Your teacher has asked you to say whether or not you think your town or city should hold such an event. Use details from the passage as well as your own knowledge to form an opinion about why a parade of this kind would be a good idea for your town or city.

Example: You read an article about a word game, how it developed, who plays it, and why it became popular. Then you are asked if you would like to play this game, and to explain why or why not.

How would I write these answers?

You will have to think about ideas and information from the article or story and use them to back up your opinion.

Remember as you write your response to connect your opinion to the story or article you have just read! That's what makes an argument or opinion much stronger.

LET'S TRY IT TOGETHER

> **DIRECTIONS:** Read this story, and answer the questions that follow.

In the story below, you will learn Rosa's opinion about school uniforms.

Debate Team

Rosa had practiced her speech at home for a solid week before today. She was the newest member of the debate team and she wanted to prove that she could argue her opinion as well as anyone else on the team. The debate she was taking part in was about school uniforms.

She believed that uniforms were a great idea for her school. She had many reasons to back up her point of view. She thought that uniforms would improve the school environment. Rosa planned to point out that she spent a lot of time in the morning trying to pick out what to wear each day. She thought that she could use that time in the morning to get more sleep or to eat a good breakfast.

Another point Rosa planned to make was that uniforms could save money for the families of the students in the school. She figured out how much money her mother spent on clothes for herself and her younger brother, and then checked the price of uniforms. It would be a huge savings for her family. ∎

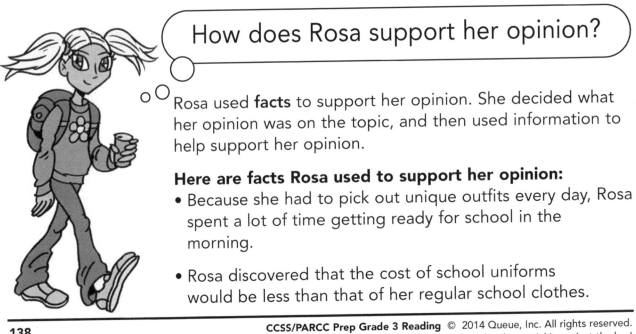

How does Rosa support her opinion?

Rosa used **facts** to support her opinion. She decided what her opinion was on the topic, and then used information to help support her opinion.

Here are facts Rosa used to support her opinion:

- Because she had to pick out unique outfits every day, Rosa spent a lot of time getting ready for school in the morning.

- Rosa discovered that the cost of school uniforms would be less than that of her regular school clothes.

RL.3.10: MAKING JUDGMENTS/DRAWING CONCLUSIONS

What does it mean to make a judgment?

Every day, every one of us makes judgments.

When you **make a judgment** about something you have read in a passage, you use what you already know together with information from the passage itself to make a decision.

Making judgments can help you to understand what you are reading.

For instance, you have learned that sometimes authors do not come out and say what they really mean. When that happens, the author is relying on the reader to make his or her own judgment about a character or about what will happen in a story.

Here are questions to ask yourself when trying to make a judgment based on a passage:

- What is important?
- Why?
- How does the author lead the reader from one event to another?
- How does each event in the story affect the rest of the story?
- What is the most likely explanation for the question at hand?

Authors tell readers much more than they come right out and say. They give you hints or clues to help you "read between the lines."

YOU TRY IT

> **DIRECTIONS:** Read the paragraph, and answer the questions that follow.

Safety is about you and it's about the bicycle. A bicycle is a vehicle. It is not a toy. Knowing how to properly ride a bicycle is a serious skill. Before you go out riding, there are things to check. Your bicycle should be the right size for you. Make sure to protect your head and always wear a helmet. All its parts should work well. The seat should not swivel and the chain should be attached properly. Your grips should be in good condition, and your handlebars should be safely tightened. If you plan to ride in the early morning, evening, or night, you should have reflectors on the front and back of the bike. The tires should have enough air in them. You want to have fun, but you want to be safe, too. ■

1. **Which of the following is the *most* important thing a bicycle rider needs to stay safe?**
   A   a basket for carrying things
   B   a helmet
   C   short-finger gloves
   D   a bell

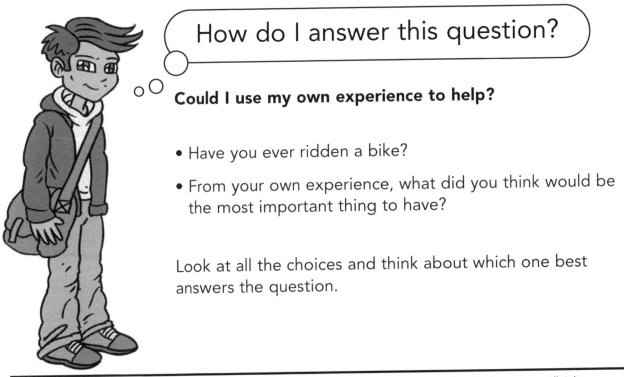

How do I answer this question?

Could I use my own experience to help?

- Have you ever ridden a bike?

- From your own experience, what did you think would be the most important thing to have?

Look at all the choices and think about which one best answers the question.

Which answer is the best?

Is it answer choice A?
Did your bike have a basket? If it did, did the basket help you to ride the bike? If not, was it more dangerous to ride without the basket?

What about answer choice B?
Do you wear a helmet when you ride a bike? Why? Would it be a good idea to wear one?

Could it be answer choice C?
Do you wear gloves when you ride a bike? Would wearing gloves keep you safe?

How about answer choice D?
Would having a bell on your bike be important? If your bike didn't have a bell, what might happen?

The most important thing for anyone riding a bicycle is safety. The question asks you to judge which choice is the most important. A helmet will help to keep a person safe, even if there is an accident, so B is the correct answer.

What does it mean to draw a conclusion?

When you **draw a conclusion**, you pull out the meaning of what you have read. The word **draw** here does not mean sketching or making a picture; it means to "pull out."

(e.g., At a county fair, a worker might draw a fairgoer's ticket from a jar and call him the winner of the raffle.)

You must have strong evidence from the story or article to draw a conclusion that makes sense.

How do I draw a conclusion?

To draw a conclusion, you want to follow several steps.

- Start by identifying the main idea and the supporting details.
- Think about what you already know about the topic.
- Then put the information from the story or article together with what you already know to draw a conclusion.

Once you have reached your conclusion, either think about what you have read or review the passage. You will want to make sure that the conclusion you have reached seems correct.

YOU TRY IT

> **DIRECTIONS:** Read this paragraph, and answer the question that follow.

Joe is with his family on vacation. Every morning they wake up to the sound of birds. One bright sunny morning, Joe is the first one out of the tent. He goes to get the food they will need for breakfast from the car. Along the way, he stops to look at the scenery before him. Joe realizes that he hadn't really paid attention to it before. He can't believe how very beautiful it is! ■

1. **What kind of vacation are Joe and his family taking?**

A a big-city tour of museums and historic sites
B a seashore holiday of swimming and sailing
C a week of camping in a large national park
D a visit to Joe's grandparents' dairy farm

How would I answer this question?

First, you should look for information within the text.

What clues do we get from the text?

- They hear sounds of birds.
- They are staying in a tent.
- There is beautiful scenery.
- Joe gets the food from the car.

Then, think about your own experiences.

What experiences could you draw from?

- Have you seen beautiful scenery?
- Where?
- Where have you heard birds?
- Have you ever stayed in a tent? If so, where were you?
- Where could you be where your food wouldn't be in a pantry or a refrigerator?

Which answer is best?

Finally, take a look at the locations mentioned in your answer options.

A a big city
Could this be the answer? Probably not. How do you know? Think about the facts we know. Most people do not stay in tents in big cities. This is probably not the correct answer.

B the seashore
This probably is not the correct answer. A seashore vacation would probably involve the beach, swimming, and sailing. None of these is mentioned in the passage.

C a national park
This could be the correct answer. At a national park, there is beautiful scenery and animals, such as birds. Also, it would make sense for a family to stay in tents at a national park. Keeping food in the car would protect it from bears and raccoons.

D a dairy farm
Even though you think that answer choice C could be the correct answer, it is important to look at all your options. A dairy farm would be a busy farm area with lots of cows and livestock. The only animals mentioned in the passage were birds. Also, if Joe is visiting his grandparents, he would most likely be staying in their house.

Putting together all the information from the passage with your own experience, you should draw the conclusion that Joe and his family are on vacation at a national park, answer choice C.

YOU TRY IT

DIRECTIONS: Read this passage, and answer the questions that follow.

Olympic Events

In the Summer Olympics, there are events involving horses and riders. These are divided into three categories: dressage, show jumping, and three-day events. Each of these events shows off the skills of riders under different conditions.

Dressage

In this event, riders perform careful moves, known as paces and halts, while riding their horses. These movements show judges how much control each rider has while on the horse. Because of the grace and rhythm of some of the motions, some people think they look similar to dancing.

The rider controls the movements with gentle hands on the reins. Different kinds of pressure from the rider's legs direct the horse in its movements. The rider's weight also influences the horse's actions.

Show Jumping

This event has two parts. In the first, the horse and rider jump over rails and stone walls. The riders try not to knock any of these down. They have to do it in a set time.

✔ **CHECKING FOR UNDERSTANDING**
What are some ways the rider can control the horses' movements?

The second event is similar to the first. The difference is that the turns are tighter and the rails and walls higher. Riders try to complete the course in the fastest time. However, they also try not to topple the rails or walls. Their scores are based on their times and how clean their rides are.

Three-Day Event

These events, held over the three days, are all done in set times.

Day 1

This is a dressage event. It is very similar to the dressage event described above.

Day 2

This is an endurance event.* It has three parts to it. The first is a ride of a few miles over roads and tracks. Then, there are high-speed steeplechase jumps. Next comes several miles riding over natural terrain. This is on roads, tracks, and cross-country. It is easy to see that a horse and rider must be very fit for this event.

Day 3

This day is for show jumping. It is like the separate show-jumping event. Coming after Day 2, when the horse may be tired, it is a very hard event. It is a good test to show which are the best horses and riders.

Horses and riders train for years to be in the Summer Olympics. Large crowds of people watch them. ∎

* An endurance event is one that requires a horse and a rider to work over a longer period of time and for longer distances. These types of events often test a horse's ability to perform well while putting forth lots of effort.

1. **What do the horses' movements look like in the dressage event?**

   A a race

   B a game

   C a swim

   D a dance

   ⭐ **HELPFUL HINT**
   This question asks you to recall a fact based on what you have read in the passage. What did the passage tell you about how the horses' movements look? If you are unsure of the answer, reread the dressage section.

2. **How does the rider tell the horse what to do?**

   A by whispering in the horse's ear

   B by gently pulling on the reins

   C by moving down in the saddle

   D by patting the horse on the head

   ⭐ **HELPFUL HINT**
   This question asks you to recall a detail from the passage. If you are unsure of the answer, reread the dressage section. You should be looking for the place where the author mentions how the rider controls the horse.

3. **What is different about the second show-jumping event?**

   A The walls are higher.

   B The event is not timed.

   C The horses are less tired.

   C The riders are not needed.

   ⭐ **HELPFUL HINT**
   This question asks you to draw a conclusion. What did the passage tell you about the second show-jumping event? If you are unsure of the answer, reread the show jumping section.

4. The horse and rider need to be fit for Day Two's events because they must

   A look nice as they perform.

   B travel long distances.

   C wait awhile for their turn.

   D move very carefully.

HELPFUL HINT

This question asks you to draw a conclusion. Can you remember what happens on Day Two? Was there anything that would require fitness? If you are unsure of the answer, reread the Three-Day Event section.

5. Why might the third day be very hard for riders and horses?

   A Both may not have been trained for show-jumping.

   B Both are tired after the second day's events.

   C The horse does not want to listen to the rider.

   D The rider forgets all the rules by this time.

HELPFUL HINT

This question asks you to recall information based on what you have read in the passage. What did the author tell you about Day 3? If you are unsure of the answer, reread the Three-Day Event section.

6. Why did the author *most likely* write this passage?

   A to show readers which event draws the most people

   B to tell readers which event riders like the best

   C to show readers how horses train for the Olympics

   D to tell readers about Olympic events for horses

HELPFUL HINT

This question asks you to make a judgment. What did this passage try to do? What have you learned from reading it?

FOR THE OPEN-ENDED QUESTION BELOW, REMEMBER TO:
• Pay attention to what the question is asking you.
• Be sure to answer everything the question asks you.
• Fully explain what you mean by your answer.
• Use details from the story.

7. Imagine that you are a rider in the three-day event.
   • How would you feel if you won the event?
   • What would you do to reward your horse for its efforts in this event?

YOU TRY IT

P.T. Barnum

Phineas Taylor Barnum was born on a farm in Connecticut in 1810. He was the oldest of five children. People called him Taylor when he was a young boy. It was the name of his grandfather. Barnum went to school until he was twelve years old. He was a good student, especially in arithmetic. However, he did not finish school. He left to help his father on the farm.

From the beginning, P.T. was different. He bargained for everything. P.T. was always trying to get things for less. While other kids were enjoying themselves, he was making money. He sold homemade candy on holidays. He bought animals and sold them to people in his town.

Barnum's life changed when he was twelve. A man asked him to help take cattle to New York City. While in the city, P.T. saw a different world. There were museums, shows, and tall buildings. P.T. knew that this was where he wanted to live. However, he had to return home to the farm.

When P.T. was 15, his father died. Barnum went to work in a local store. He was now the sole supporter for his family. In a short time, the owners allowed him to run the store. He started a lottery. Green bottles were the prizes. The people loved it even though they knew the prizes were worthless. They liked the way Barnum ran the lottery. It was fun just to play. This taught P.T. a lesson he never forgot: People don't mind being fooled if they can have fun.

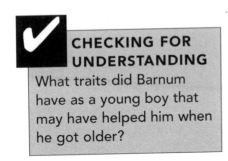

CHECKING FOR UNDERSTANDING

What traits did Barnum have as a young boy that may have helped him when he got older?

Barnum had a number of jobs over the next few years. In each job he worked for someone else. Then P.T. started his own candy store in his hometown. He also started another lottery. He put ads in newspapers to sell lottery tickets. No one had done this before. Many tickets were sold. P.T. learned that advertising was a good way to make money. Then, in 1834, things changed. His business failed. P.T. thought he would try his luck in New York City. This is where he had always wanted to go.

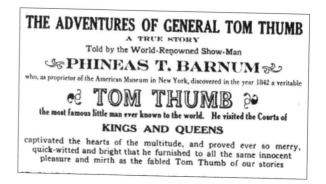

THE ADVENTURES OF GENERAL TOM THUMB
A TRUE STORY
Told by the World-Renowned Show-Man
PHINEAS T. BARNUM
who, as proprietor of the American Museum in New York, discovered in the year 1842 a veritable
TOM THUMB
the most famous little man ever known to the world. He visited the Courts of
KINGS AND QUEENS
captivated the hearts of the multitude, and proved ever so merry, quick-witted and bright that he furnished to all the same innocent pleasure and mirth as the fabled Tom Thumb of our stories

One day, he saw an unusual show. A woman claimed to be 161 years old. P.T. felt that people would love this show and he asked the woman to join him. The woman agreed. He put ads in local newspapers telling people about his new show. Soon many people were coming to see the woman. This was the first of several shows owned by P.T. Barnum.

P.T. bought the American Museum in 1841. He made it the most exciting museum in the city. His acts included Siamese twins and unusual animals. He even had a little person called "Tom Thumb." Many people came to the museum.

By 1850, P.T. Barnum had become rich. He sold the museum and moved back to his hometown. He built a big house and also started a circus. In 1856, P.T. again lost his money. He had to sell his house. P.T. and Tom Thumb went on a tour of Europe. When he came back, P.T. bought the American Museum again.

Sadly, the American Museum burned. P.T. decided to start another circus. He called it the "Greatest Show on Earth." In this circus, he added sideshows. These were small tents near the big tent. Unusual stunts were done in each one. People paid more money to see these stunts. People loved these sideshows.

P.T. died in 1891. Right up until the time of his death, he was involved in developing acts. People said that he was the greatest showman of his time. P.T. Barnum spent his entire life working hard and spreading joy. ■

1. **What does the word "developing" mean in the last paragraph?**

   A rushing

   B joining

   C watching

   D forming

HELPFUL HINT
This question asks you to select the meaning of the word "developing". Reread the sentence in the paragraph that uses the underlined word. Are there any clues in the other sentences from that paragraph to the word's meaning?

2. **Why did P.T. Barnum leave school?**

   A to work at a local store

   B to visit New York City

   C to help his father farm

   D to join the nearby circus

HELPFUL HINT
This question asks you to recall a detail from the passage. If you are unsure of the answer, reread the early paragraphs from the passage. You should be looking for where the author mentions Barnum leaving school.

3. **When did P.T. Barnum use the lesson that he had learned about advertising in newspapers?**

   A to get people to see the 161-year-old woman

   B to buy the American Museum in 1841

   C to open sideshows with his circuses

   D to travel to New York City with cattle

HELPFUL HINT
This question asks you to determine an answer from what the passage has said. After P.T. Barnum learned about advertising in newspapers, how did he use that information?

4. **What did seeing New York City do for P.T. Barnum?**

   A It made him want to own a store.

   B It made him want to see Europe.

   C It made him happy to live on a farm.

   D It made him want to move there.

HELPFUL HINT

This question asks you to recall a detail from the passage. How did P.T. Barnum feel about New York City? If you are unsure of the answer, reread the third paragraph of the passage.

5. **How was P.T. Barnum different from other people who ran lotteries?**

   A He ran the lottery in a candy store.

   B He told people about the lottery in the newspaper.

   C He gave away green bottles as prizes for the winners.

   D He ran the lottery in Connecticut.

HELPFUL HINT

This question asks you to draw a conclusion. What did P.T. Barnum do to let a lot of people know about the lottery? If you are unsure of the answer, reread the fifth paragraph.

6. **Why did P.T. Barnum think people would love the 161-year-old woman?**

   A They would not be impressed.

   B They would be amazed.

   C They would be afraid.

   D They would read the newspaper.

HELPFUL HINT

This question asks you to guess based on what you have read in the passage. Why do you think P.T. Barnum decided to have the woman be a part of his show? If you are unsure of the answer, reread the sixth paragraph.

FOR THE OPEN-ENDED QUESTION BELOW, REMEMBER TO:
- Pay attention to what the question is asking you.
- Be sure to answer everything the question asks you.
- Fully explain what you mean by your answer.
- Use details from the story.

7. **How would you describe P.T. Barnum's personality and character? Use details from the passage to support your answer. Think about including details about his childhood, schooling, and businesses.**

YOU TRY IT

> **DIRECTIONS:**   Read this passage, and answer the questions that follow.

Lipizzaner Horses

A special breed of horse is the Lipizzaner. This breed has a long and interesting history. They come mostly from crossing Andalusian and Arabian horses. These horses were from Spain and North Africa. Over the years, six special stallions have changed the breed. Some of these horses were brought from Spain to the town of Lipizza. This is how Lipizzaner horse got their name.

A Lipizzaner is a rather small, powerful horse. It has short legs and a very strong body. At birth, foals are usually black or brown. Later, their color changes to almost white. They are gentle and intelligent. The Lipizzaner was a favorite horse of wealthy noble people. It is a riding and show horse. Some are seen in circus acts.

There is a Spanish Riding School for these horses in Austria. Lipizzaner horses are trained to perform special dressage programs there. Only stallions are used. For the first four years, the colts are free to play and graze. Then, their training begins. This takes about four years. The horse and rider learn many steps, jumps, and spinning moves. Thousands have seen them perform.

During World War II, Lipizzaner horses were in great danger. Colonel Alois Podhajsky, of the Spanish Riding School, was in charge of the training of these animals. He feared for the horses' safety. The Nazis wanted the shows to go on in Vienna, Austria. They wanted to show that they were winning the war. However, with all the bombing, the horses might be seriously hurt. So, the colonel smuggled some of them away.

CHECKING FOR UNDERSTANDING
Why would this breed of horse be used for circus acts?

Only ten horses and two riders were left to keep up the show. When air raid horns sounded (which warned people of attacks by armed planes), these horses would automatically lie down. Even though they were shaken, they behaved well. Finally, these horses were secretly taken to safety.

At the close of the war, more Lipizzaner horses from other countries were brought together. This kept the breed and the school going. It took ten years for them to get back to their school site in Vienna.

In 1955, the school gave its first show since the end of the war. This show took place 320 years after the school had opened. The Lipizzaners continue to live and to perform. ■

1. **How did the Lipizzaner horses get their name?**

   A from the man who rescued them

   B from the town where they were bred

   C from the show in which they performed

   D from the training they were given

HELPFUL HINT
This question asks you to recall a detail from the passage. Can you remember where the story mentioned the origin of the Lipizzaner name? If you are unsure of the answer, reread the first paragraph.

2. **The purpose of the second paragraph is to**

   A explain why Lipizzaners were in danger.

   B show where Lipizzaners came from.

   C tell about the tricks Lipizzaners can do.

   D describe what Lipizzaners look like.

HELPFUL HINT
This question asks you to find a detail in the passage based on the way the text is organized. Reread the second paragraph. Why do you think the author wrote the paragraph? What did it tell you?

3. **Which horses are used during shows?**

   A only the colts

   B only the brown horses

   C only the gentle horses

   D only the stallions

HELPFUL HINT
This question asks you to recall a detail from the passage. If you are unsure of the answer, reread the third paragraph. You should be looking for where the author mentions which horses are used for the shows.

4. **Why did the horses *most likely* lie down when air raid horns sounded?**

   A The loud noises frightened them.

   B It is what they were trained to do.

   C Their riders were also lying down.

   D They thought it was time to sleep.

HELPFUL HINT
This question asks you to draw a conclusion. For what reason would the horses lie down when they heard a loud noise? Do you have animals? How do they react to loud noises? Why?

5. **Why did Colonel Alois Podhajsky want to take the horses out of Austria?**

   A He thought he could make more money in Spain.

   B He wanted to let people everywhere see the horses.

   C He wanted to keep the horses safe during the war.

   D He thought that he should go someplace warmer.

HELPFUL HINT
This question asks you to figure something out based on what you have read in the passage. Was there a specific reason why the colonel would want to take the horses out of Austria? If you are unsure of the answer, reread the fourth paragraph.

6. **Why did the author *most likely* write this passage?**

   A to tell the history of the Lipizzaners

   B to tell where Lipizzaners can be seen

   C to tell what a Lipizzaner rider must learn to do

   D to tell how to take care of Lipizzaners

HELPFUL HINT
This question asks you to make a judgment about the passage. Why would the author choose to write this passage? What did you learn from reading it?

FOR THE OPEN-ENDED QUESTION BELOW, REMEMBER TO:
• Pay attention to what the question is asking you.
• Be sure to answer everything the question asks you.
• Fully explain what you mean by your answer.
• Use details from the passage.

7. Lipizzaner horses are a special breed, which makes them unique in certain ways. However, they also share many characteristics with horses we see around on farms and in cities in this country. Think about what you know about Lipizzaner horses and about horses you might see more often in this country.

   • How do you think they are alike?

   • How do you think they are different?

Use at least two details from the passage to answer each question.

YOU TRY IT

Wishes and Dreams

"Chris, are you ready yet?" his dad calls. "Be sure to take a jacket. It will be cool when the sun goes down."

"I'm coming," Chris answers. With that, he comes bounding down the stairs. He's wearing his baseball cap and a football jersey. It has a big number 15 and his favorite team's quarterback's name on it. He has his football tucked under his arm. "Bye, Mom," he says as they give each other a hug and a kiss.

"Bye, Chris, have a good time. See you tonight. I hope your team wins," his mother says.

Chris Barber and his dad, Vern, are off to pick up Marty Hamilton and his son, Tyrone. Ty and Chris are best friends and in the same class at school. They are also teammates on one of the town's Pop Warner League football teams.

4 | Ty and his dad are standing outside their home waiting as Mr. Barber and Chris pull up. Chris and Ty greet each other as Chris gets out of the car. Chris opens the back door and helps Ty with his backpack and jacket. Then, they both climb into the back seat. Marty adds their cooler and bags of food to what Vern already has in the trunk.

✔ **CHECKING FOR UNDERSTANDING**
Why do you think the author told us all about the travel and time before the game? How does that fit in the story?

They are soon on their way to the stadium. The gates open a few hours before 1:00 p.m. That gives the men time to break out the portable gas grill and get ready to cook some food.

While their dads get busy preparing lunch, the boys start tossing the football. It isn't long before some other kids join them. They play three against three. Chris plays quarterback for his team. He tosses a wobbly pass, and Ty makes a mad dash to catch it. The ball lands close to a group tailgating nearby. One of the men tosses it back to Ty.

The game goes on for some time. There is a lot of action—some great catches and runs for touchdowns. Ty and Chris hear Vern calling, "Boys, come on, the burgers and dogs are ready."

After eating, they pack up and walk to the stadium. They go through security and then up the escalator to their seats in the upper tier.

The game is exciting. Their team wins by a field goal in the last two minutes! Chris and Ty consider this a great day. On the way home they talk about some of the players and the plays they made.

"I can't decide if I want to be a quarterback or a wide receiver," Ty says.

"Why don't you be a wide receiver and I'll be the quarterback?" Chris suggests. "I think I have a good arm and you're a faster runner."

Their fathers just laugh. "I think you have a few years to decide those things," Chris' father says. "You're still a bit young. You have a lot of growing up to do. Who knows? You might get to be a big lineman."

"In the meantime, just enjoy the game," Marty advises.

Both fathers had played football in college. They were good, but not good enough to make the pros. They wanted to be in the National Football League. Neither one ever dreamed of being a lawyer or an accountant. That's what they are, though. Now their boys have the same dreams that their dads had when they were that age. Who's to say? Maybe there will be a Hamilton or a Barber in the NFL after all. ∎

1. **What is this passage *mostly* about?**

   A two dads who teach boys to play football

   B two boys who don't want to go to a game

   C two boys who want to be football players

   D two dads who are famous football players

HELPFUL HINT
This question asks you to find the central idea of the passage. If you are unsure of the answer, skim over the passage. Think about what information is crucial to the story.

2. **The purpose of the fourth paragraph is to**

   A describe things the boys like to do on weekends.

   B show the two boys working and playing together.

   C tell the reader how to join a Pop Warner team.

   D tell the reader how Ty and Chris know each other.

HELPFUL HINT
This question asks you to find a detail in the story based on the way the text is organized. Reread the fourth paragraph. Why do you think the author wrote the paragraph? What did it tell you?

3. **Who wants to be a quarterback?**

   A Ty

   B Chris

   C Ty's dad

   D Chris's dad

HELPFUL HINT
This question asks you to recall a detail from the story. Which of the boys wanted to be a quarterback? If you Are unsure of the answer, skim the passage.

4. **What do the dads do before the game?**

   A coach a team

   B play football

   C prepare lunch

   D work as lawyers

   ⭐ **HELPFUL HINT**
   This question asks you to remember what the passage has said. What were the dads doing before the group went to the stadium to watch the game? If you are unsure of the answer, reread the sixth paragraph.

5. **What helps to make it a great day for Chris and Ty?**

   A Their dads teach them to play football.

   B They eat hamburgers and hot dogs.

   C They join a football team together.

   D Their team wins a football game.

   ⭐ **HELPFUL HINT**
   This question asks you to guess based on what you have read in the passage. What in the story made the day even better for Chris and Ty? If you are unsure of the answer, reread the first half of the story.

6. **Why does Chris's dad say that the boys might become linemen?**

   A to say that the boys still have a lot of growing up to do

   B to warn the boys that they will grow up too quickly

   C to tell the boys which teams they played for in college

   D to help the boys think about other football jobs

   ⭐ **HELPFUL HINT**
   This question asks you to draw a conclusion. Why do you think Chris's dad said what he did? What did he really mean? If you are unsure, reread the end of the passage.

FOR THE OPEN-ENDED QUESTION BELOW, REMEMBER TO:
• Pay attention to what the question is asking you.
• Be sure to answer everything the question asks you.
• Fully explain what you mean by your answer.
• Use details from the story.

7. At the end of this passage, Chris's father warns the boys about planning too far ahead. We then learn that both fathers had wanted to be in the NFL, but instead became a lawyer and an accountant. Why do you think a person should try to get a good education even if he or she could be very, very good at sports someday?

YOU TRY IT

The Magic Show

People of all ages love to watch a magic show. It has humor, excitement, and suspense. Audiences see things that seem impossible. Rabbits are pulled from an empty hat or pieces of string suddenly become one long rope. Everyone knows that what they are seeing is not possible; yet they enjoy every minute of the show.

2   The modern magic show began in the mid-1850s with Robert-Houdin. He brought magic tricks to theaters. Before Houdin, magicians performed their tricks before small crowds of people outside. These early shows were usually short. When the show was over, the magicians moved to the next town. Houdin, however, put together an entire evening of magic tricks. The people loved these magic shows. They were so successful that other magicians began to imitate Houdin's shows.

Large magic shows became popular in both Europe and America. Each magician did something different. Harry Houdini performed many daring escapes as part of his show. Percy Tibbles walked through brick walls on stage. Harry Blackstone made horses disappear. Due to the popularity of these shows, books on how to do magic tricks soon appeared. The modern magic show was here to stay.

An audience watching magic shows knows that what they see is not real. Cut string does not become a rope again, people do not disappear and reappear, and rabbits do not live in hats. Even though people know that these tricks are not real, they usually cannot explain how the tricks are done.

Many people think magic tricks use special props or equipment. Yes, many magic tricks do require special props. However, the most important part of any trick is the magician. He or she is an actor who pretends to do the impossible. His or her key job is to keep people from noticing what is being done on stage. This is called the "psychology of deception."

Good magicians talk the entire time they are on stage. This magician talk is called "patter." Patter draws people's attention away from what the magician is doing to complete the trick. Often, magicians will explain things in great detail. When they do this, people think they are explaining the trick. However, that is not true.

A magician talks for two reasons. The first is to control what people look at during the trick. Through speaking, the magician causes people to look at the wrong things. This prevents them from noticing what is actually being done.

For example, the magician may say, "Remember, you need to keep your eyes on the cup with the ball under it." The magician then moves the cups rapidly around the table. People try to follow the cup with the ball.

However, that cup will move only once or twice. It will be the other cups that are moved many times. The people will not be able to find the ball because they have been following all the other cups. This causes them to lose track of which cup the ball is actually under.

The second reason for talking is to confuse people. People become so involved in what the magician is saying that they forget to look carefully at what is actually happening. They miss what is being done.

Timing is also important in magic shows. There are two reasons that magicians focus on timing. The first is to build suspense. Each time the magician does something during a trick, the suspense builds. This leads people to want to know what will be done next. Some tricks take a long time to complete. Good magicians build suspense during each part of the trick.

The second purpose of timing is to confuse people. For example, sleight-of-hand tricks must be done slowly. However, the magician will speak of the quickness of the hand while doing this type of trick. This makes the people look for quick hand movements. They then miss the slow easy motions by which the trick is done. Good magicians are masters at using timing to mask what they are doing.

Magic tricks used in today's shows fall into five groups. Sleight-of-hand tricks involve the skillful use of hands. Things appear and disappear from the magician's hands in these tricks. An example of this type of trick involves small balls. The magician will make these balls appear, disappear, and change size. He does this while putting them under inverted cups or dishes.

Close-up magic is a second group of tricks. These tricks are usually done on a table, with people standing close to the magician. Making coins appear under objects on a table is an example of this type of trick.

Illusions are a third type of magic trick. This is where large objects seem to change or disappear. An example is sawing a person in half. A person is placed in a box with his or her head and feet sticking out. Then, the magician seems to saw the person in half. After he is finished sawing, he opens the box. The person just sawed in half steps onto the stage. These tricks involve special equipment.

Making impossible escapes is a fourth type of magic trick. Here a magician escapes from what looks like an escape-proof place. He is first placed in an escape-proof cell. Then someone makes sure that the ropes or chains are secure. The cell is then covered. The magician proceeds to free himself or herself from the ropes or chains.

The last group involves mind-reading tricks. In these tricks, the magician seems to reveal to people what they are thinking.

The success of magic lies in the ability to do things that appear real. Most people know that the tricks are not real. Yet, they enjoy watching the magician perform tricks because of the excitement and mystery surrounding the show. ■

1. **The purpose of the second paragraph is to**

   A show how each magician is different.

   B tell about early magic shows.

   C show how magicians confuse people.

   D tell where to see the best magic.

HELPFUL HINT

This question asks you to find a detail in the passage based on the way the text is organized. Reread the second paragraph. Why do you think the author wrote the paragraph? What did it tell you?

2. **What does the word "imitate" mean in paragraph two?**

   A watch

   B plan

   C copy

   D write

HELPFUL HINT

This question asks you to select the meaning of the word "imitate." Reread the sentence in paragraph two that uses the word. Are there any clues to the word's meaning in the other sentences in that paragraph?

3. **What do *most* people watching a magic show know?**

   A how to do the magic trick

   B that the trick is not real

   C how the magician fools them

   D that the magician is not happy

HELPFUL HINT

This question asks you to guess based on what you have read in the passage. What do you think most of the people in the audience would think? What do you recall about what the author said about this?

4. **What do good magicians always do on stage?**

  A talk

  B dance

  C walk

  D sing

HELPFUL HINT

This question asks you to recall a detail from the passage. If you are unsure of the answer, reread the sixth paragraph.

5. **What is the second reason that magicians watch their timing?**

  A to make people excited

  B to make sure people are laughing

  C to make people puzzled

  D to make sure people are watching

HELPFUL HINT

This question asks you to find a detail in the passage based on the way the text is organized. When the passage talks about timing, what was the second reason magicians pay attention to the timing? If you are unsure of the answer, reread that part of the passage.

6. **Each time a magician does something during a trick, the audience**

  A moves closer to the stage.

  B looks to see what time it is.

  C figures out how the trick works.

  D tries to guess what will be done next.

HELPFUL HINT

This question asks you to recall what the author has said in the passage. What do you think the audience is trying to do during a magic trick? What would you be trying to do?

FOR THE OPEN-ENDED QUESTION BELOW, REMEMBER TO:
• Pay attention to what the question is asking you.
• Be sure to answer everything the question asks you.
• Fully explain what you mean by your answer.
• Use details from the passage.

7. What is the purpose of patter? Use information from the passage to support your response.

_____

_____

_____

_____

_____

_____

_____

_____

_____

_____

_____

_____

_____

_____

_____

Made in the USA
Charleston, SC
24 June 2014